16 MORE Extraordinary African Americans

Nancy Lobb

PHOTO CREDITS

Jesse Owens: Athlete	© 1936 Associated Press
Benjamin O. Davis Jr.	Photo courtesy of U.S. Air Force
Fannie Lou Hamer	© 1965 Associated Press
Coretta Scott King	© 2003 Associated Press/Ric Feld
Alex Haley	Photo courtesy of Alex Haley
Muhammad Ali	© Muhammad Ali Enterprises
Faith Ringgold	Photo provided by Faith Ringgold
Alice Walker	© 2008 Associated Press/John Amis
Gladys Knight	© 2007 Associated Press/Eric Risberg
Bernice Johnson Reagon	© Andrew Zuckerman
Colin Powell	Photo courtesy of State Department
Benjamin Carson	© Fritz Photography
Morgan Freeman	© 2008 Associated Press/Danny Moloshok
Geoffrey Canada	Photo courtesy of Harlem Children's Zone
Ruth Simmons	Photo courtesy of Brown University

The classroom teacher may reproduce materials in this book for classroom use only. The reproduction of any part for an entire school or school system is strictly prohibited. No part of this publication may be transmitted, stored, or recorded in any form without written permission from the publisher.

1 2 3 4 5 6 7 8 9 10
ISBN 978-0-8251-6504-7
Copyright © 2009
J. Weston Walch, Publisher
40 Walch Drive • Portland, ME 04103
www.walch.com

Printed in the United States of America

Contents

To the Teacher v

To the Student vii

Langston Hughes: Poet 1

Jesse Owens: Athlete 9

Benjamin O. Davis Jr.: Tuskegee Airman 17

Fannie Lou Hamer: Voter Registration Activist 25

Coretta Scott King: Civil Rights Leader 33

Alex Haley: Author 41

Muhammad Ali: Boxer 48

Faith Ringgold: Artist 56

Alice Walker: Author 64

Gladys Knight: Singer 71

Bernice Johnson Reagon: Singer/Educator/Artist 79

Colin Powell: Statesman/Soldier 86

Benjamin Carson: Physician 94

Morgan Freeman: Actor 102

Geoffrey Canada: Social Activist 110

Ruth Simmons: University President 118

Vocabulary 125

Answer Key 129

Additional Activities 137

References 142

To the Teacher

According to *Reading Next: A Vision for Action and Research in Middle and High School Literacy*, a report to the Carnegie Corporation of New York (2004, second edition), "High-interest, low-difficulty texts play a significant role in an adolescent literacy program and are critical for fostering the reading skills of struggling readers and the engagement of all students. In addition to using appropriate grade-level textbooks that may already be available in the classroom, it is crucial to have a range of texts in the classroom that link to multiple ability levels and connect to students' background experiences."

Biographies about extraordinary people are examples of one such kind of text. The 16 Americans described in this collection should both inspire and reassure students. As students read, your instruction can include approaches that will support not only comprehension, but also learning from passages.

Reading and language arts skills not only enrich students' academic lives but also their personal lives. The *Extraordinary Americans* series was written to help students gain confidence as readers. The biographies were written to pique students' interest while engaging their understanding of vocabulary, recalling facts, identifying the main idea, drawing conclusions, and applying knowledge. The added value of reading these biographies is that students will learn about other people and, perhaps, about themselves.

Students will read stories demonstrating that great things are accomplished by everyday people who may have grown up just like them—or maybe even with greater obstacles to overcome. Students will discover that being open to new ideas, working hard, and believing in one's self make them extraordinary people, too!

Structure of the Book

The Biographies

This collection of stories can be used in many different ways. You may assign passages for independent reading or engage students in choral reading. No matter which strategies you use, each passage contains pages to guide your instruction.

At the end of each passage, you will find a series of questions. The questions are categorized, and you can assign as many as you wish. The purposes of the questions vary:

- **Remembering the Facts:** Questions in this section engage students in a direct comprehension strategy, and require them to recall and find information while keeping track of their own understanding.

- **Understanding the Story:** Questions posed in this section require a higher level of thinking. Students are asked to draw conclusions and make inferences.

- **Getting the Main Idea:** Once again, students are able to stretch their thinking. Questions in this section are fodder for dialog and discussion around the extraordinary individuals and an important point in their lives.

- **Applying What You've Learned:** Proficient readers internalize and use the knowledge that they gain after reading. The question or activity posed allows students to connect what they have read to their own lives.

In the latter part of the book, there are additional resources to support your instruction.

Vocabulary

A list of key words is included for each biography. The lists can be used in many ways. Assign words for students to define, use them for spelling lessons, and so forth.

Answer Key

An answer key is provided. Responses will likely vary for Getting the Main Idea and Applying What You've Learned questions.

Additional Activities

Extend and enhance students' learning! These suggestions include conducting research, creating visual art, exploring cross-curricular activities, and more.

References

Learn more about each extraordinary person or assign students to discover more on their own. Start with the sources provided.

To the Student

> When the history books are written in future generations, the historians will have to pause and say, "There lived a great people—a black people—who injected new meaning and dignity into the veins of civilization."
> —Dr. Martin Luther King Jr.

The lives of many African Americans have made a difference in the story of America. Writers, artists, scientists, teachers, politicians, ministers, lawyers, doctors, businesspeople, athletes, and so many more, have helped to make America what it is today. African Americans can be proud of their heritage. It is a pride all Americans should share.

In *16 Extraordinary African Americans*, you read the story of sixteen of these people. In *16 MORE Extraordinary African Americans*, you will read the stories of sixteen more outstanding black Americans. They are:

- Langston Hughes, a poet whose poems tell the story of Black America

- Jesse Owens, an athlete who won fame at the 1936 Olympic Games

- Benjamin O. Davis Jr., a pilot who led the Tuskegee airmen in World War II

- Fannie Lou Hamer, a sharecropper who became a symbol of the voter registration drives of the 1960s

- Coretta Scott King, wife of Dr. Martin Luther King Jr. who became a civil rights hero in her own right

- Alex Haley, whose book *Roots* gave African Americans pride in their heritage

- Muhammad Ali, three-time heavyweight boxing champion of the world

- Faith Ringgold, an artist who is best known for her story quilts

- Alice Walker, a writer who won the Pulitzer Prize for her novel *The Color Purple*

- Gladys Knight, a singer who has had #1 hits in pop, gospel, and rhythm & blues

- Bernice Johnson Reagon, founder of the gospel group Sweet Honey in the Rock

- Colin Powell, a four-star general who was the first black Secretary of State

- Benjamin Carson, a pediatric neurosurgeon who has saved the lives of many very ill children

- Morgan Freeman, an actor who has played many outstanding roles

- Geoffrey Canada, CEO of the Harlem's Children Zone

- Ruth Simmons, a teacher who became the first black president of an Ivy League university

The motto on the Great Seal of the United States reads "E PLURIBUS UNUM." That is Latin for "Out of many, one." The United States is made up of many peoples of many races. These peoples have come together to form one nation. Each group has been an important part of American history. I hope you will enjoy reading about sixteen African Americans who have made a difference.

—Nancy Lobb

Langston Hughes

Poet

My People

The night is beautiful,
So the faces of my people.

The stars are beautiful,
So the eyes of my people.

Beautiful, also, is the sun,
Beautiful, also, are the souls
of my people.

—Langston Hughes

Langston Hughes is one of the greatest American poets. He has been called the "poet laureate of the Harlem Renaissance." Hughes wrote about life as he knew it in the early 20th century. He wrote about injustice and the struggle for black civil rights. His poems tell the stories of Black America. They sing with the feelings of blues, jazz, and spirituals.

James Mercer Langston Hughes was born on February 1, 1902, in Joplin, Missouri. He was an only child. His father, James, was studying to be a lawyer. But then a law was passed that only whites could take the bar exam. James became bitter. He left the family and moved to Mexico soon after Langston was born.

After this, Langston's mother moved from city to city looking for work. She left Langston with his grandmother in Lawrence, Kansas. Langston felt he had been abandoned by his parents. He grew up a lonely child. He began writing poems as a way to express his feelings.

When Langston was 13, his grandmother died. He stayed with friends for the next two years. Then he went to live with his mother, who had re-married. They lived first in Illinois and then in Cleveland, Ohio. Then his mother and stepfather moved to Chicago. Langston did not go with them. At 15, Langston lived by himself in a rented room and went to school.

Langston attended Central High School in Cleveland for four years. He was an excellent student. He was on the track team. He was also on the staff of the school magazine, the *Monthly*. He began writing poems and stories for the *Monthly*. Most of his poems were about how it felt to be black.

When Langston was 17, his father asked him to come live with him in Mexico. Langston was thrilled for the chance to get to know his father. But, the two did not get along at all. Langston soon returned to Cleveland.

Langston graduated from high school in 1920. He decided that he wanted to go to Columbia University. He wanted to become a writer. But first he would have to go back to Mexico and ask his father for money.

Langston got on the train bound for Mexico. As he sat, he watched the Mississippi River out the window. The river made him think about the flow of his life. His mind drifted to what rivers had meant in the history of black people. He began writing a poem on the back of an envelope. That poem was "The Negro Speaks of Rivers." It was the poem that would later bring fame to Langston Hughes.

The Negro Speaks of Rivers

I've known rivers:
I've known rivers ancient as the world and older than
the flow of human blood in human veins.

My soul has grown deep like the rivers.

I bathed in the Euphrates when dawns were young.
I built my hut near the Congo and it lulled me to sleep.
I looked upon the Nile and raised the pyramids above it.

I heard the singing of the Mississippi when Abe Lincoln went
down to New Orleans, and I've seen its muddy bosom turn all
golden in the sunset.

I've known rivers:
Ancient, dusky rivers.

My soul has grown deep like the rivers.

James Hughes was a practical man. He was willing to pay for Langston to go to college. But he would not pay for him to study poetry. He worried that Langston could not make a living as a poet. He wanted Langston to study engineering instead.

Langston refused to do this. Instead, he got a job. He also began sending poems to *The Brownies' Book*. This was a new magazine for black children. Within a few months, Langston had published several poems, a play, an essay, and some short stories in the magazine.

Then "The Negro Speaks of Rivers" was published in a magazine for adults called *The Crisis*. The founder of this magazine was W. E. B. DuBois, a civil rights activist.

When James Hughes saw the success his son was having, he gave in. He sent him to New York to attend Columbia University. Langston spent just a year at Columbia. Then he decided to travel and see the world.

He got a job on a freight ship headed for Africa. He hoped to learn more about his roots. Next, he worked on a ship going to the Netherlands. Finally, he ended up in Paris.

In 1924, Hughes returned to New York City. He was surprised to learn he was well-known as a poet. At this time in the 1920s in the Harlem neighborhood of New York, much black music and art was created. Blues and jazz became popular. The time was known as the "Harlem Renaissance."

Hughes met other famous writers of the Harlem Renaissance. Among his friends were Zora Neale Hurston, Countee Cullen, and James Weldon Johnson. In 1926, Hughes published his first book of poems, *The Weary Blues*.

Hughes decided to return to college. He enrolled at Lincoln University in Pennsylvania. While there, he published a second book of poems. In 1929, he graduated from college. That same year, the stock market crashed. This was the beginning of the Great Depression. Many people lost their jobs. Instead of spending time on music and art, people had to focus on survival. The Harlem Renaissance abruptly ended.

In the 1930s, Hughes became interested in writing plays. He and Zora Neale Hurston wrote the play *Mule Bone*. He wrote nine other plays in his lifetime. (Many of these plays were published after his death.) In 1935, his play *Mulatto* became the first play by a black writer to appear on Broadway. He also published a novel based on his life called *Not Without Laughter*.

During the 1930s, Hughes lived in different places in the United States. He also traveled abroad. In the 1940s, Hughes moved back to Harlem. He lived there for the rest of his life. Soon after arriving, he wrote a book of poems called *Shakespeare in Harlem*.

During World War II, Hughes wrote about equality for blacks in the military. He wrote ads encouraging people to buy war bonds. He also wrote newspaper stories about the war.

Hughes also wrote many more poems. Race was the common theme of his poems. In 1951, his epic poem *Montage of a Dream Deferred* was published. It painted a picture of life in Harlem. One theme in the poem is equal rights. The poem describes what happens when hopes and dreams, such as civil rights, are put off until a later time.

Harlem

What happens to a dream deferred?

Does it dry up
Like a raisin in the sun?
Or fester like a sore—
And then run?
Does it stink like rotten meat?
Or crust and sugar over—
Like a syrupy sweet?

Maybe it just sags
Like a heavy load.

Or does it explode?

In 1960, Hughes received the Spingarn Medal. The award is given out by the National Association for the Advancement of Colored People (NAACP). This is the highest award for an African American who performs "acts of distinguished merit and achievement." The next year, Hughes was inducted into the National Institute of Arts and Letters.

On May 22, 1967, Langston Hughes died. His funeral was held in Harlem. A jazz band played. Some of Hughes's poems were read. It was a celebration of the life of a remarkable man. The section of 127th Street where he lived in Harlem has been renamed Langston Hughes Place.

In 2002, a U.S. postage stamp was issued to honor Hughes. That same year, a cover story in *The Crisis* showcased Hughes and his work. Langston Hughes is still a proud voice for African-American freedom. Part of his poem "I Dream a World" reads:

> I dream a world where black or white,
> Whatever race you be,
> Will share the bounties of the earth
> And every man is free.

Remembering the Facts

1. Why did Langston's father become bitter?

2. Why did Langston begin writing poems as a child?

3. What is the theme of the poem "The Negro Speaks of Rivers"?

4. Why did Langston's father decide to pay for him to study writing at Columbia?

5. What was the Harlem Renaissance?

6. Name two writers Hughes met in Harlem.

7. How did Hughes work for black rights during World War II?

8. What is a theme of *Montage of a Dream Deferred*?

Understanding the Story

9. How do you think Langston Hughes's poems show what it was like to be black?

10. In the poem "Harlem," Hughes writes about what happens when people cannot achieve their dreams. What do you think Hughes says could be the cost of not being able to follow your dreams?

Getting the Main Idea

In what ways do you think Langston Hughes is a good role model for all Americans?

Applying What You've Learned

Write a short poem in the style of Langston Hughes. Your subject should be something you know well and feel strongly about.

Jesse Owens

Athlete

Jesse Owens won fame at the 1936 Summer Olympic Games in Berlin, Germany. He became known as the fastest man in the world. He was a symbol of the best in American athletics.

He was born James Cleveland Owens on September 12, 1913, in Oakville, Alabama. He was called by his initials, J.C. He was the youngest of ten children.

The Owenses earned their living by sharecropping. Sharecroppers farmed another person's land for a share of the crop earnings. Half the money went to the land owner. The Owens family kept the other half. This was barely enough money to keep the family in clothing and food.

J.C. was a small, sickly child. He had bad colds and got pneumonia each winter. The Owenses' house had no central heating system. Mrs. Owens wrapped J.C. up in old feed sacks. She kept him near the woodstove.

By the time J.C. was six years old, he was well enough to go to school. The Owens children walked nine miles to a one-room school for blacks. J.C. learned to read and write but not much else.

From a young age, J.C. loved to run. He has said, "It was something you could do all by yourself, and under your own power. You could go in any direction, fast or slow as you wanted, fighting the wind if you felt like it, seeking out new sights just on the strength of your feet and the courage of your lungs."

When J.C. was nine, the Owens family moved to Cleveland, Ohio. They hoped to find a better life. Mr. Owens worked in a steel factory. Mrs. Owens cleaned houses and did laundry for other families. All the children had jobs, too.

J.C. went to Bolton Elementary School. On his first day at school, the teacher asked his name. She could not understand his Southern accent. She wrote down his name as "Jesse." He did not correct her. For the rest of his life, he was known as Jesse.

Jesse entered Fairmount Junior High in 1927. There he met two people who changed his life. The first was Ruth Solomon. The two dated through junior high and high school. Later, they were married. The second was Charles Riley, the track and field coach.

Riley saw right away that Jesse could be a great runner. Jesse had a job after school. Riley began working with Jesse every morning before school. The rest of the team practiced in the afternoon.

Riley became like a second father to Jesse. He made sure Jesse ate well. He told Jesse he must push himself to the limit every day. He taught Jesse always to look to the future. He had Jesse work for steady improvement. He trained Jesse to run every race to beat his own best times.

One day, Riley took Jesse to a race track to watch the horses run. They studied how the horses seemed to run with no effort. Their hooves barely touched the ground. Their eyes looked straight ahead. They seemed to fly gracefully over the ground. Jesse changed his running style to be more like that of a race horse. He was so successful that other runners everywhere later copied him.

In Jesse's first year on the track team, he broke the world junior-high records for the high jump and the long jump. Jesse decided then that he would work to reach the Olympics.

Jesse went to East Technical High School in 1930. Coach Riley continued to work with him. Jesse won race after race. He tried out for the 1932 Olympic track team during his junior year. But he did not make the team.

In the summer of 1932, Jesse and Ruth Solomon were secretly married. Later that year, their daughter, Gloria, was born. Jesse supported his new family at first with various odd jobs. Ruth quit school to work in a beauty shop. She lived with her parents, who helped her care for the child.

Jesse went on with his senior year of high school. He didn't lose a race all year. He was elected student body president. Racial equality was lacking during this time in U.S. history. As a black man in a school where 95 percent of his classmates were white, this was amazing.

The National Interscholastic Meet was held in June 1933. Jesse tied the world record for the 100-yard dash. In the 220-yard dash he set a new world record. Cleveland honored him with a parade when he got home.

It was not surprising that many colleges wanted to sign Jesse Owens. He decided to go to nearby Ohio State University (OSU).

Jesse faced racial inequality every day at OSU. He was not allowed to live on campus because he was black. He got a room a mile away. He worked as an elevator operator at the statehouse to earn money. But he had to run the freight elevator in back. The front elevators were run by white athletes.

Jesse's coach at OSU was Larry Snyder. Snyder taught him to smooth out his stride and how to get a faster start. Snyder taught Jesse to pump his arms and legs in the long jump. This helped Jesse sail farther through the air. He worked hard. On May 25, 1935, it paid off.

That day, the Big Ten Track and Field Championship was held in Ann Arbor, Michigan. Five days earlier, Jesse Owens had fallen and hurt his back. Snyder wanted him to withdraw from the meet. But Owens would not quit.

His first event was the 100-yard dash. For the second time in his life, he tied the world record of 9.4 seconds. Then he set a new world record in the long jump (26 feet 8 inches). Next, he set a new world record in the 220-yard dash. To cap off the day, he set another world record in the 220-yard low hurdles. In one day, Jesse Owens had broken three world records and tied a fourth. Jesse Owens was a star.

Owens began to train hard for the Olympics. He easily earned a spot on the team. On July 15, 1936, he left college and set sail for Germany. He wore the only suit he owned. That didn't matter. His dream of going to the Olympics had come true.

Germany in 1936 was ruled by Adolf Hitler. He was the head of the Nazi party. The Nazis believed that black people were not as good as white people. Hitler hoped the Olympic Games would prove his belief that white Germans were superior. He watched the Games with interest from his box.

On August 2, 1936, Jesse Owens ran his first race, the 100-meter run. He blasted out of the starting block. He won the race in 10.3 seconds. The German runner finished fifth. Owens tied the world record. He had his first gold medal.

In spite of the Nazis' beliefs, the German people loved Jesse Owens. They stood and cheered each time he ran. Owens even became close friends with a white German athlete named Luz Long.

In the long jump, Owens won his second gold medal. He sailed through the air 26 feet 5 ½ inches. It was a new Olympic record. Luz Long took the silver. After the race, the two men shook hands. They walked past Hitler's box together. Pictures of the two men shaking hands became the symbol of the 1936 Olympics.

The next day was the 200-meter run. Again Owens won gold. His time was another Olympic record of 20.7 seconds.

Next came the 400-meter relay. The U.S. team won that race in world-record time. That was a fourth gold medal for Jesse Owens. He had competed in four events and won gold in all four. He had also tied or set new Olympic and/or world records in all four events. The American team won more medals in track and field than any other country.

The Olympics came to a close. Owens looked forward to running in the Olympics in the future. The next Olympics were to be in 1940 in Japan. But World War II put an end to both the 1940 and the 1944 Olympics. Owens would never compete in another Olympics.

Owens returned home from Germany at the end of the summer of 1936. He was honored with parades and parties. But soon reality set in. He would have to earn a living. He tried many different jobs with little success. He became a bandleader. He owned a traveling basketball team. He formed a softball league. And he started a dry-cleaning business. He couldn't make enough money to support his wife and three daughters with any of these jobs.

He found that he enjoyed giving speeches. He founded a public relations company and sponsored products. He did very well with this business.

In 1950, the Associated Press named Owens the greatest track-and-field athlete in history. He began to travel for the U.S. State Department as a goodwill ambassador. He also promoted athletics for young people living in poverty.

Owens continued these activities for the next 20 years. He also wrote a number of books. One of these was his autobiography. It was called *The Jesse Owens Story.*

In 1972, he received an honorary degree from Ohio State University. He was inducted into the Track and Field Hall of Fame in 1974. In 1976, President Gerald Ford gave him the Presidential Medal of Freedom. And in 1979, President Jimmy Carter gave him the Living Legend Award.

Owens and his wife retired to Arizona. But his retirement was short. He died of lung cancer on March 31, 1980. In his honor, the Jesse Owens Foundation was created to help young people.

Jesse Owens was remembered around the world after his death. The track stadium at OSU was named for him. President George H. W. Bush presented Ruth Owens with the Congressional Gold Medal in Jesse Owens's name. Even a street outside the Olympic stadium in Berlin was named Jesse Owens Strasse.

Remembering the Facts

1. What is sharecropping?

2. Why did Jesse say he loved to run?

3. Name two pieces of advice Coach Riley gave Jesse.

4. How did Jesse end his high-school track career?

5. In which events did Jesse set new world records at the Big Ten meet?

6. Why did Hitler watch Owens's Olympic races with great interest?

7. Why did Owens never race in another Olympics?

8. What honor did the Associated Press give Owens in 1950?

Understanding the Story

9. Why do you think the picture of Owens and Long shaking hands became a symbol of the 1936 Olympics?

10. Why do you think it is important that a street in Berlin was named after Jesse Owens?

Getting the Main Idea

Why do you think Jesse Owens is a good role model for young people today?

Applying What You've Learned

Owens once said, "The only victory that counts is the one over yourself." Explain what you think he meant.

Benjamin O. Davis Jr.
Tuskegee Airman

The Tuskegee Airmen were the United States military's first black pilots. Before 1940, some people thought blacks did not have the ability for combat. The Tuskegee Airmen proved them wrong. The Airmen were a highly decorated all-black squadron of World War II fighter pilots. Benjamin O. Davis Jr. was their leader.

Davis graduated from West Point military academy. He was the first black in the 20th century to do so. He was the first black four-star general. Davis's successful career pushed the armed forces to integrate in 1948.

Benjamin O. Davis Jr. was born on December 18, 1912, in Washington, D.C. His mother sewed clothes at home to earn money. His father, Benjamin O. Davis Sr., served in the U.S. Army for 50 years. Benjamin had two sisters. His mother died after giving birth to his younger sister. Benjamin was just five years old.

Benjamin's father found that blacks were limited to a few jobs in the army. Blacks were not allowed to command white soldiers. So Benjamin Sr. spent much of his career teaching military science at black colleges. He also led black ROTC (Reserve Officers' Training Corps) units.

When Benjamin was eight, his father re-married. The family moved to Tuskegee, Alabama. Tuskegee Institute was a college for blacks. His father taught and led the ROTC units there.

The family moved to Cleveland, Ohio, when Benjamin was 12. His father commanded some black army regiments there.

When Benjamin was 14, he and his father took a trip. They went to Washington, D.C., to see family. He asked his father to take him to Bolling Field. This was a small dirt airfield. Barnstormers flew in and out of the field. A barnstormer was a pilot who made a living doing stunt flying. Barnstormers also gave rides and flying lessons.

Benjamin's father gave him $5 for a ride. (This was a lot of money then.) The plane was small. It had an open cockpit. Benjamin wore goggles and a helmet. He later said, "About all I really remember are the takeoff and the feeling of (excitement) at being in the air, looking down on the city of Washington and up at white clouds far above us. And I remember a sudden surge of (desire) to become a (pilot)." This was a turning point in his life.

Benjamin went to Central High in Cleveland. He finished at the top of his class at the age of 16. He was also student council president.

Benjamin went on to Western Reserve University. He studied math. He also tried the University of Chicago. He found he was bored. He wanted an army career like his father had. He wanted to go to West Point. (This military academy trains officers for the U.S. Army.)

It has always been very hard to get into West Point. Students who want to attend need high grades. They have to be very strong and fit. They must prove their leadership skills. They also have to be nominated by a member of Congress.

At that time, no white Congressman would nominate a black student. But there was one black Congressman. He was Oscar De Priest of Illinois. De Priest nominated Benjamin. He entered West Point on July 1, 1932.

Benjamin was one of two non-white cadets at West Point. Still, Benjamin thought he would be accepted by his peers. He soon found out he was very wrong.

The first summer was Cadet Basic Training. All the new cadets had a rough time. They were not allowed to walk anywhere. They had to "double time" instead. They had to stand at attention for hours. At meals, they had to keep their eyes on their plates at all times. As they ate, they were drilled on facts they had memorized.

But it was worse for Davis than for the other cadets. He was "silenced" by everyone because he was black. Not one person on campus spoke to him outside the line of duty. Davis never had a roommate. No one would eat with him. He was "the invisible man" on campus. This went on for four years!

The other cadets hoped he would quit. But Davis only worked harder. In 1936, he graduated. He was 35th in a class of 276. He was the first black in the 20th century to graduate from West Point. (Three others had graduated in the 1800s.)

Davis did earn the respect of his white classmates. This is shown by the words under his yearbook picture: "The courage, tenacity, and intelligence with which he conquered a problem (far) more difficult than the first year (at the academy) won him the admiration of his classmates. His single-minded (work) to continue in his chosen career cannot fail to inspire respect."

Davis was glad to leave West Point. He hoped to be trained as a pilot in the Army Air Corps. But he soon was disappointed. He would not be admitted to flight school because he was black.

Davis married Agatha Scott in 1936. Then he reported for duty to Fort Benning, Georgia. He was put in charge of the 24th Infantry Division. But again Davis was discriminated against. Not one white officer welcomed Davis. He was not even allowed to enter the Officers' Club.

At that time, black troops were not trained for combat. The 24th Infantry Division's job was "service." They cleaned the white officers' quarters. They kept the equipment running. They kept the grounds mowed and trimmed. This work insulted Davis. It did not use his training. But Davis did his best at the job.

From 1937 to 1938, Davis attended Infantry School. White officers who finished this type of training were given command of an active regular army regiment. But Davis was sent to Tuskegee Institute to teach instead. Davis knew this was the army's way of getting him out of their way. Davis spent 2 ½ years at Tuskegee. He had little to do there. He said it was "as close to nothing as it could be and still be called a job."

In 1940, things began looking up. President Franklin Roosevelt ran for re-election. He made efforts to gain support from black voters. He made Benjamin's father a brigadier general. General Davis was the first black general in U.S. military history. Roosevelt also ordered the Army Air Corps to form a black flying unit. It would be called the 99th Fighter Squadron.

In 1941, Benjamin Davis was chosen as one of 12 members of the first black pilot training class. He reported to Tuskegee Army Air Field. There was a lot riding on this first class. If they did well in combat, there might be more options for blacks in the military.

Davis loved flight school. On his first few flights, the instructor sat in the captain's seat. He controlled the plane as Davis watched. Soon Davis got to handle the controls himself. Davis said, "Flying was one great feeling!"

The training went on for seven months. In March 1942, Davis and four others earned their wings. From 1942 to 1946, nearly 1,000 more black Tuskegee Airmen earned theirs.

On December 7, 1941, the Japanese bombed Pearl Harbor, a U.S. naval base in Hawaii. The United States entered World War II. Many pilots were needed in the fight.

Davis and the 99th Fighter Squadron went to North Africa. They flew their first mission on June 2, 1943. Many more missions followed. Sometimes they flew a dozen missions a day. They bombed railroad yards, bridges, factories, and airfields.

The work of the 99th was outstanding. As a result, two larger black fighter groups were formed. These were the 332nd Fighter Group and the 477th Bombardment Group. Davis was assigned to lead the 332nd.

The job of the 332nd was to protect B-24 bombers as they hit German targets. One day, 39 of Davis's fighters held off more than 100 German fighter planes! Another time, Davis led eight American fighters in an attack on 18 German fighter planes. The 332nd never lost a single bomber they were escorting.

The Tuskegee Airmen shot down 111 enemy planes. They destroyed 150 planes on the ground. They destroyed more than 950 boxcars and trucks. They sunk more than 40 boats. They even sunk a German destroyer. (No one else had ever done this.) They only lost 66 American planes.

The Tuskegee Airmen flew nearly 15,000 missions over territory held by the Germans. Davis himself led many of these. He was awarded the Silver Star and the Distinguished Flying Cross.

The war ended in 1945. Davis returned to the United States. He was given command of the 477th Bombardment Group. He was also the base commander of Lockbourne Army Air Base. Both blacks and whites were under his command. This was the first time an air base had been led by a black officer. A report on Lockbourne called it "the best-managed base in the Air Corps."

In 1947, the Air Force became a separate branch of the service. In 1948, all the armed forces were ordered to be integrated. The Air Force was the first branch of the services to do so. There is no doubt this was due to the work of Davis and the Tuskegee Airmen.

Over the next 20 years, Davis had many other important assignments. In 1953, he commanded the 51st Fighter-Interceptor Wing. This group flew missions during the Korean War. In 1965, he was chief of staff for American forces in South Korea. He became a three-star general. Later he led the 13th Air Force in the Philippines. In 1968, he became assistant commander of the U.S. Strike Command in Florida.

In 1970, Davis retired from the Air Force. He had served 33 years. Next he headed the federal sky marshal program. He also was assistant secretary at the U.S. Department of Transportation. In 1991, he published his autobiography. He named it *Benjamin O. Davis, Jr.: American.*

In 1998, President Bill Clinton awarded Davis a fourth star. This made him a full general.

General Benjamin O. Davis Jr. died on July 4, 2002. At his funeral, a World War II fighter plane flew overhead. President Clinton said, "General Davis is proof that a person can overcome [hard times] and discrimination, achieve great things…and [shows how] one person can bring [great] change."

The motto of West Point is "duty, honor, country." Benjamin O. Davis Jr. lived up to that motto. He met many challenges in his life. Yet he kept going. He said he wanted "to make things easier for those who would come after" him. He was determined to succeed in his chosen field despite all the odds against him…and he did.

Remembering the Facts

1. What did Benjamin's father do at Tuskegee Institute?

2. When did Benjamin decide to become a pilot?

3. Name three reasons life at West Point was hard for Davis.

4. What did the 24th Infantry Division do at Fort Benning?

5. Why was Davis allowed to enter pilot training?

6. What was the job of the 332nd Fighter Group?

7. How many bombers were lost while under escort by the Tuskegee Airmen?

8. Name an award received by Davis.

Understanding the Story

9. Why do you think the title of Davis's autobiography tells much about him?

10. Explain how Davis helped to integrate the armed forces.

Getting the Main Idea

In what ways do you think Davis is a good role model for young Americans?

Applying What You've Learned

Imagine being Davis as a West Point cadet. Make a list of words that would describe your feelings.

Fannie Lou Hamer
Voter Registration Activist

Fannie Lou Townsend Hamer was poor and had little education. She worked most of her life growing and picking cotton in Mississippi. But Fannie Lou wanted to be able to vote. Yet she couldn't because she was black. She fought to get this right for herself and others. She became a symbol of the voter registration drives of the 1960s. In the end, she did win the right to vote. She also gained the respect of people around the world.

Fannie Lou Townsend was born on October 6, 1917, in Montgomery County, Mississippi. Her parents, Jim and Ella Townsend, had 20 children. Fannie Lou was the youngest. Her parents were paid $50 upon Fannie Lou's birth. At that time, the owners of the plantation where they worked thought of babies as future field hands.

When Fannie Lou was two, her family moved to Sunflower County, Mississippi. They worked as sharecroppers, growing and picking cotton.

The Townsend family was large, so they grew and picked a lot of cotton. But they still earned very little money. One year, Jim Townsend did get a little ahead. He bought three mules, a wagon, and some tools. But one night a white neighbor poisoned the mules. He didn't like to see a black family having so much success.

After the cotton harvest was over, the Townsends would walk through the fields. They would gather leftover scraps of cotton. It took a lot of walking to "scrap" together a bale of cotton. Ella sold the scrapped bale. She used the money to buy food for her family. Still, there was rarely enough to eat. Dinner might have been greens and flour gravy. Other nights they had onions and bread.

The family lived in a wooden shack. It had no running water. There was no electricity or indoor plumbing. In the winter, there was no central heating system. The children had no shoes. Ella would tie her children's feet in sacks. This way they wouldn't freeze.

When Fannie Lou was six years old, she had polio. This was a serious disease that left some patients with lifelong muscle weakness or paralysis. For the rest of her life, Fannie Lou walked with a limp.

There was little schooling for children who farmed. School started in December after the cotton harvest. It ended in March when planting began. Fannie Lou loved to go to school when she could. She especially liked spelling and reading.

In sixth grade, Fannie Lou had to leave school. She had to help her family work in the fields. She read when she could. Sometimes she would read newspapers or magazines that other people had thrown away.

The church was an important part of Fannie Lou's life. She joined the Strangers Home Baptist Church. She was baptized in the Quiver River. She read her Bible every day.

Her mother taught her at home, too. She said that hatred made a person weak. Ella taught her to be a good person and to respect herself.

Singing was an important part of black culture. Songs were sung to pass the time, as prayer, and to tell stories of the past. From an early age, Fannie Lou loved to sing. She learned hymns and spirituals in church. Years later, she sang civil rights songs. Famous folk singers such as Harry Belafonte and Pete Seeger were amazed at the power of her voice.

Fannie Lou's brothers and sisters moved to the North when they grew up. They hoped to find work and a better life. Fannie Lou stayed behind to take care of her parents.

In 1944, Fannie Lou Townsend married Perry Hamer. The couple lived in a small house on the Marlow plantation near Ruleville, Mississippi. Fannie Lou washed clothes. She picked cotton. She cooked and cleaned. The couple enjoyed fishing for catfish or perch when they had free time. They later adopted two daughters.

In August of 1962, Fannie Lou Hamer went to church. The preacher talked about a mass meeting. It would be held at the church the next night. Hamer went to the meeting. It was led by workers from the Student Nonviolent Coordinating Committee (SNCC—pronounced "snick"). They wanted to help black people register to vote.

Hamer was amazed. She did not know that by law, any adult American citizen (black or white) had the right to vote. In order to vote, people had to register.

In Mississippi at that time, the white community made it difficult and often dangerous for black people to vote. First, blacks had to pass a "literacy test." They had to "read and interpret" the state constitution. They had to do this to the satisfaction of the white registration clerk. Because few blacks were able to go to school for very long, few passed the literacy test.

Those who did pass had to pay a poll tax. This money had to be paid before a person could vote. Few blacks could afford to pay.

There were other ways many whites kept blacks from voting. The Ku Klux Klan threatened to hurt blacks if they didn't stay "in their place." These were violent times for blacks living in the South.

At the end of the mass meeting, the SNCC workers called for volunteers to register to vote. Fannie Lou Hamer, 45 years old, was the first person to raise her hand. It was a dangerous decision. But Hamer later said, "The only thing they could do to me was to kill me. It seemed like they'd been trying to do that a little bit at a time ever since I could remember."

The volunteers had to go to the courthouse in Indianola to register. On August 31, 18 blacks rode in a bus to Indianola. They filled out voter registration applications. Then they took the literacy test. They all failed, including Hamer.

She began singing hymns on the way home. She sang "Go Tell It on the Mountain" and "This Little Light of Mine." Her singing gave the group courage. It also showed Hamer's belief that the civil rights struggle was a deeply spiritual issue.

When Hamer got back home, there was a message waiting for her. The voting clerk had called her boss, Mr. Marlow. He said she must withdraw her application to vote. If she didn't, she would be fired.

Hamer left the plantation that very night. She went to stay with friends in nearby Ruleville. A few days later, 16 shots were fired into the home where she was staying.

In December, Hamer and her husband moved into a small house in Ruleville. Both had lost their jobs. They had no money. Hamer had nearly lost her life. All this was because she had tried to register to vote.

Hamer went back to the courthouse in Indianola. She told the voting clerk: "Now, you can't have me fired because I'm already fired. I won't have to move now because I'm not living in a white man's house. I'll be here every 30 days until I become a registered voter!" One month later, she passed the test.

Hamer still couldn't vote. She had to save enough money to pay the poll tax. The Ku Klux Klan tried to scare her off, too. Night after night, they drove by her house with guns. She wouldn't back down.

In 1963, Hamer began working for SNCC. One day in June, she and a group of others went to a meeting in Tennessee. On the way back, they stopped and tried to get something to eat. They were arrested because the restaurant was only for whites. While she was in jail, Hamer was badly beaten. She never fully recovered. She became more determined to continue her work to register other blacks to vote.

She traveled around the South. She spoke at mass meetings. She went to northern states to raise money for SNCC. And in spite of her limp, she walked in civil rights marches around the country.

Hamer was a powerful speaker. At one meeting she said, "It's time to question things. You always hear … that it takes time to change things. For 300 years, we've given them time. I've been tired so long that I'm sick and tired of being sick and tired!"

She was also a powerful singer. She sang all the time, wherever she went. She sang in jail. She sang at meetings and sit-ins. Her voice gave people courage. This was her favorite song:

> This little light of mine,
> I'm going to let it shine.
> Let it shine,
> Let it shine,
> Let it shine.

Hamer said the song meant: "Let your light so shine that men see your good works and glorify the Father which is in heaven." She also said, "I think singing is very important. It brings out the soul."

In 1964, the Democratic party of Mississippi was nearly all-white. Hamer helped found the Mississippi Freedom Democratic Party (MFDP). The MFDP had black and white members. In 1964, delegates from both parties tried to be seated at the Democratic National Convention in Atlantic City.

Hamer spoke for the MFDP on national television. She told viewers what happened to blacks in the South when they tried to vote. People across the nation were horrified. However, only two of the MFDP delegates were seated as official delegates. The others were allowed to stay as honored guests of the convention.

Hamer's work helped make big changes. In 1965, the Voting Rights Act was passed. This law said that states could not use literacy tests to stop a person from voting. Then in 1966, another law made the poll tax illegal. These were important victories in the civil rights struggle.

By the next Democratic National Convention things were improving. The convention was held in Chicago in 1968. Hamer was seated as an official delegate from a black-and-white delegation from Mississippi.

For her work in voter registration, Hamer received many honors. In 1969, she received an honorary doctorate from Morehouse College. In 1971, she was elected to the Central Committee of the National Women's Political Caucus.

Hamer went back to the town of Ruleville. There she worked to help the poor, both black and white. She helped get a low-cost day-care center for the town. She worked for better housing. She even raised money to start a farm co-op. At the co-op, low-income people who didn't own farmland could grow crops for food.

In 1976, the people of Ruleville joined together to honor Hamer. They had a special "Fannie Lou Hamer Day."

Hamer died on March 14, 1977. Many famous people came to pay their respects. The service had to be held in the Ruleville High School gym to hold all the people. One of the speakers was Andrew Young. He was the U.S. ambassador to the United Nations. Young was the first African American to hold this post. He said, "None of us would have been where we are now, had she not been there then."

Hamer was born poor. She didn't have a formal education. She did stand up and sing out for what she believed. Hamer let her light shine for all the world to see. As she did, she helped win the right to vote for her people.

Remembering the Facts

1. How did Fannie Lou try to learn after she stopped going to school?

2. Why were Fannie Lou's parents paid $50 at her birth?

3. Name three reasons it was hard for southern blacks to register to vote.

4. List two things that happened to Hamer because she tried to register to vote.

5. What work did Hamer do for SNCC?

6. Why was the Mississippi Freedom Democratic Party formed?

7. What happened at the 1968 Democratic National Convention?

8. Name three things that Hamer did to help the low-income people of Ruleville, Mississippi.

Understanding the Story

9. Explain why you think singing was an important part of black culture.

10. Why do you think "This Little Light of Mine" was Fannie Lou Hamer's favorite song?

Getting the Main Idea

In what ways do you think Fannie Lou Hamer is a good role model for young people today?

Applying What You've Learned

Imagine you are a young black person in the 1960s in the South. You are trying to register to vote. Write a paragraph telling about your feelings.

Coretta Scott King
Civil Rights Leader

Coretta Scott King was the wife of Dr. Martin Luther King Jr. Dr. King was killed on April 4, 1968. Mrs. King continued his work. She became an important civil rights leader in her own right. She devoted her life to justice for all.

Coretta Scott was born on April 27, 1927, in Heiberger, Alabama. Heiberger was a small farming town. It was mostly black. Coretta's parents were Obadiah and Bernice Scott. They raised their three children in a two-room house on the family farm. The children were Coretta, her older sister, Edythe, and her younger brother, Obie.

Coretta grew up during the Great Depression. The Scotts worked hard to get by. Obadiah worked in a sawmill. He hauled logs during the day. At night he worked as a barber. He cut hair in his home. The children had to do the chores. They tended the crops on the farm.

By the age of ten, Coretta was working for neighbors in their cotton fields. She dug, chopped, and picked cotton for months. If she was lucky, she might earn $5 for the entire season. This was good money during the Depression.

In the fall, Coretta and Edythe walked three miles to school. Two black teachers taught more than 100 black children. Grades one to six were all in one room. Coretta used the money she earned picking cotton to buy her books. In contrast, white children in town rode to school on a bus. Class sizes were smaller. White children got their books for free.

Coretta learned about racism at a young age. Her father worked hard. He saved his money. He bought a truck and a sawmill. Some white men didn't like this. They burned Obadiah Scott's sawmill down. When Coretta was ten, Obadiah bought a larger home for his family. The whites burned that down, too. The white sheriff wouldn't even investigate.

When she was 12, Coretta went to Lincoln Normal School in Marion, Alabama. Lincoln was a private school. It had been started by recently freed slaves after the Civil War to educate blacks. It was run with the help of white missionary teachers from the North. All the students were black. At Lincoln, Coretta learned to read music. She learned to play the piano and the trumpet.

Coretta graduated first in her class. She won a scholarship to Antioch College in Yellow Springs, Ohio. She majored in elementary education and music.

After receiving her degree, Coretta won a scholarship to the New England Conservatory of Music in Boston. She studied concert singing and violin. She worked several jobs to pay her living expenses. Coretta worked so hard that she didn't have time to meet many people.

One day, a friend called her. He said that he had mentioned her name to a young black man from Atlanta. The young man was a Ph.D. student in theology (religious studies) at Boston University. His name was Martin Luther King Jr. He wanted to meet her.

Coretta agreed to have lunch with him. She was not impressed with King. She thought he was too short. Plus, she had no interest in marrying a minister. But Martin Luther King Jr. had decided on that first date that he would marry Coretta.

The two began dating. Martin made no secret of the fact that he wanted to marry her and raise a family. He also wanted her to put him, their marriage, and family at the center of her life.

Coretta wanted to be an opera singer. She wanted to travel the world. But she had also fallen in love with King. Less than a year later, in 1953, the two were married.

After their marriage, the couple finished their studies. Dr. Martin Luther King Jr. had many job offers. Churches in both the North and the South wanted to hire him. The couple knew it would be easier to stay in the North. Life in the South at that time was hard for blacks.

The couple wanted to help blacks earn civil rights. They could have a bigger impact if they returned to the South. Dr. King accepted a job at the Dexter Avenue Baptist Church in Montgomery, Alabama.

In Alabama, blacks had to use separate restrooms and drinking fountains. They were not allowed in "white" restaurants. They had to enter buildings using separate doors. Blacks had to sit in the back seats on the city buses. If no seats were left, they had to stand or get off the bus.

On December 1, 1955, things began to change. A black woman named Rosa Parks would not give up her bus seat to a white man. She was arrested and jailed. Dr. King organized a bus boycott to protest. For more than a year, no blacks rode the city buses of Montgomery.

Many whites were angry about the boycott. One night, a woman threw a bomb into the Kings' house. No one was hurt. But the family was frightened. Coretta told Martin to stand fast and continue the boycott.

Finally, in November 1956, the U.S. Supreme Court decided on the issue. It ruled that separating whites and blacks on city buses was a violation of the U.S. Constitution. Nonviolent protest had won. Blacks around the country wanted Dr. King to help organize more protests. The time had come for blacks to push hard for their civil rights.

The civil rights movement grew. Dr. King became the leader of the Southern Christian Leadership Conference (SCLC). The goal of the SCLC was to win civil rights. The group planned marches and demonstrations across the South.

The Kings moved to Atlanta. Dr. King became the co-pastor with his father at the Ebenezer Baptist Church. His family lived on his small salary. He took no money from the SCLC.

Dr. King worked around the country for the SCLC. Mrs. King usually stayed home with their four young children. Sometimes she traveled to give "Freedom Concerts." In these concerts, she told the story of the civil rights movement in song. All the money she raised went to civil rights work.

In 1963, the largest peace march in history took place in Washington, D.C. Dr. King gave his famous "I Have a Dream" speech. Mrs. King listened as he spoke. She said it felt like "heaven itself had opened up." In 1964, Dr. King was awarded the Nobel Peace Prize.

Coretta knew her husband was in danger as the head of the civil rights movement. Each time he left the house, she knew that she might never see him again. Many people in the South did not want blacks to have equal rights. They became very violent. Martin was attacked many times. He was also arrested.

The Kings were afraid. But they knew they were doing the right thing. They continued their work. Martin had told Coretta many times that he knew his life would be cut short. He said that it wasn't how long one lived that was important. It was how well one lived. On April 4, 1968, Dr. Martin Luther King Jr. was shot and killed in Memphis, Tennessee. Riots broke out all across the country.

Coretta Scott King was a strong woman. She did not want her husband's dreams to die with him. The day before his funeral, she took his place in the civil rights march he had planned to lead in Memphis. She did the same with other events he had planned. She even spoke at a peace rally in New York using his notes.

Coretta Scott King wanted Dr. King's legacy to live on. In 1968, she established the Martin Luther King, Jr. Center for Nonviolent Social Change in Atlanta. The Center is part of a 23-acre national historic park. It teaches about human rights and freedom. Visitors see exhibits about Dr. King's life. Other exhibits tell about his teachings. Both his birth home and his final resting place are at the Center.

Mrs. King guided the creation of the King Center Library and Archives. It is the largest collection of documents from the civil rights movement. The library works to promote further understanding about the movement and nonviolence. It is also a base for creating educational materials.

Today, more than 650,000 people a year go to the King Center. The King Center and Library are Coretta Scott King's greatest legacy. She was president of the Center until 1994. Her son, Dexter King, then took over.

In 1969, Mrs. King published a book about her life called *My Life with Martin Luther King, Jr.* That same year, the American Library Association set up the Coretta Scott King Book Award. Two awards are given each year. They go to an African-American author and an African-American illustrator of a children's book. The winners' work must "promote understanding and appreciation of the culture of all peoples and their contribution to the realization of the American dream."

During the 1970s, Mrs. King's influence grew. Politicians asked her advice. They wanted her to endorse their campaigns.

Coretta Scott King worked to make Dr. King's birthday a national holiday. This dream came true in 1986. Martin Luther King Jr. Day is held every year on the third Monday in January. Mrs. King hoped that Americans would use this day for giving back to their communities.

Coretta Scott King carried the message of nonviolence and human rights around the world. She led goodwill missions to many countries. She participated in many rallies for peace and justice.

Mrs. King received honorary doctorates from over 60 colleges and universities. She wrote three books. She helped found dozens of groups that work for human rights.

Coretta Scott King died on January 30, 2006. President Bill Clinton said, "Coretta Scott King was an extraordinary woman. When her husband was taken from her, she carried on his efforts to bring America together, not knowing whether her struggle would succeed but sure that it was too important not to try." Coretta Scott King made the world a better place for all.

Remembering the Facts

1. How did Coretta Scott learn about racism at a young age?

2. What were some differences between schools for black children and schools for white children when Coretta was a child?

3. What main subjects did Coretta study in college?

4. Why did the Kings return to the South?

5. How did Coretta Scott King raise money for the SCLC?

6. What is the purpose of the King Center in Atlanta?

7. What is the Coretta Scott King Book Award?

8. What did Coretta Scott King hope Americans would do on Martin Luther King Jr. Day?

Understanding the Story

9. During the civil rights movement, why do you think some whites were against equality for blacks?

10. Coretta Scott King carried on her husband's work. Why do you think she is important in her own right?

Getting the Main Idea

In what ways do you think Coretta Scott King is a good role model for all Americans?

Applying What You've Learned

Make a list of issues you think Coretta Scott King would be involved with today.

Alex Haley
Author

As a boy, Alex Haley spent a lot of time listening to his grandmother. She could tell family stories for hours. When he grew up, he spent 12 years researching these same tales. He traveled 500,000 miles across three continents to do it. The result was his book *Roots: The Saga of an American Family*.

In *Roots*, Haley traced his roots back through slavery to Africa. No African American had ever been able to do this before.

Alex Haley was born on August 11, 1921, in Ithaca, New York. He was the oldest of three children. When he was a baby, his parents took him to Henning, Tennessee. He grew up near his grandparents, Will and Cynthia Palmer.

Alex's grandparents shaped the course of his life. Cynthia gave Alex a love for family history. Will taught Alex that hard work brings reward. These values stayed with Alex all his life.

When Alex was five, Will died. Cynthia's five sisters came to stay with her. The women spent all summer rocking on the porch. They told Alex the stories of Chicken George, Miss Kizzy, Kunta Kinte, and others from the family's past. The women also spoke words in an African language.

Alex's mother died when he was ten. Two years later, his father remarried. Alex never got over these two events. He and his father began having trouble getting along.

Alex was a gifted student. He finished high school at 15. He left home and headed for North Carolina. He spent two years at Elizabeth City Teachers College. After that, Alex wasn't sure what he wanted to do with his life. He quit school. He joined the Coast Guard. His plan was to spend three years seeing the world. Then he would return to college.

In the Coast Guard, Haley worked as a messboy and ship's cook. He was assigned to the large cargo ship the U.S.S. *Murzin*. It sailed the southwest Pacific Ocean. He was at sea for months at a time. Haley found this very boring. It was not the exciting life he had imagined.

Haley began to read everything he could find. Soon he had read all the books on the ship. Next he began to write letters. He sent long letters to everyone he knew. He hoped they would write back.

His shipmates asked him to write love letters for them to send to loved ones. This gave him the idea that he could write love stories. He sent his stories to *True Confessions* and *Modern Romances* magazines. None of the stories sold. Soon Haley had a big pile of rejection letters.

The officers on the ship learned of Haley's writing talent. They began giving Haley office work. It was a welcome break from the mess hall.

In 1941 at age 19, Haley married Nannie Branch. The couple later had two children. This marriage ended after 23 years. A second marriage also ended in divorce. Haley blamed his work for both divorces. At the time of his death, he was separated from his third wife.

While at sea, Haley became interested in the history of the Coast Guard. He heard many tales of its heroic rescues. He began writing Coast Guard adventure stories. In 1949, he sold three Coast Guard stories to *Coronet* magazine.

In fact, the Coast Guard gave Haley his start as a writer. In 1945, he was named the editor of *Our Post*. This was the official Coast Guard publication. In 1952, the Coast Guard created a job as Chief Journalist for him. He wrote stories to promote the Coast Guard in the media. Haley retired from this job in 1959.

Haley knew he had a talent for telling a good story. He decided to try to make a living as a writer.

Haley moved to New York City in 1959. *Reader's Digest* asked him to write a series of biographies. One of his first biographies was on Malcolm X. Malcolm X was a civil rights activist. Haley's article was "Mr. Muhammad Speaks." In it, Haley showed great skill as an interviewer. After that, he received many requests to write magazine articles.

Haley came up with a new interview style. He would tape the person being interviewed. He would let them talk as long as they wished on a question. The interview was then published as it had been taped. This free-flowing interview style is still popular today.

In 1962, Haley was asked to interview Malcolm X again. The interview was very successful. Grove Press asked Haley to follow up and write a book about Malcolm X. Over the next year, the two men spent hours talking. *The Autobiography of Malcolm X, As Told to Alex Haley* was published in 1965. Malcolm X did not live to read it. He was shot and killed just two weeks after the book was finished.

In 1964, Haley signed a contract to write a book about his own family history. He said it would be "a (story) of how an American Negro family rooted itself in this country over a 200-year period." He planned to trace his history back through slavery to Africa.

Haley decided to start with his grandmother's stories. He would put them together to tell his family's story. It sounded simple. It turned out to be a huge job.

Haley worked on the book for 12 years. He researched the U.S. National Archives. He searched the Library of Congress. He looked in other libraries. All the people and events he had heard about from his grandmother were written down in official records.

Haley realized that his research did not go far enough back. He needed to tell the story of how his family came to America as slaves. To do this, he would have to find out where they had lived in Africa so long ago.

Haley wondered where to start this search. He thought that the African words spoken by his grandmother could be a clue. He worked for a very long time to identify the language. Finally, he found a man who knew some of the words. The words were from the Mandingo people. The Mandingo lived in Gambia, Africa.

Haley traveled to Gambia. There he learned that the name Kinte was the name of a Gambian family. This was another clue to his history.

Haley also learned about the village storytellers. These men knew the history of their villages by heart. They knew every marriage, birth, and death. The storytellers could tell their stories for days on end.

Haley was not able to find a storyteller who knew the story of his branch of the family. He returned to the United States. Just weeks later, a friend wrote and said he had found the storyteller Haley sought. Haley had no money for another trip to Africa. The owners of *Reader's Digest* agreed to help. They gave him $300 a month plus travel expenses.

Haley traveled to Juffure, a tiny village in Gambia. He sat down with the storyteller. The old man began reciting lists of births and deaths. At last, he began telling the old story of Omoro Kinte. Omoro had four sons. The oldest son, Kunta Kinte, had gone out to chop wood one day. He was never seen again. He had been kidnapped by slavers. He was taken by ship to America. Haley knew this was the story of his family. At last, he had found his African roots.

Haley flew to London. He searched through records from old slave ships for six weeks. At last, he found the name of the slave ship on which Kinte had been held. It had sailed from Gambia to Annapolis, Maryland, in 1767.

Haley returned to the United States. He searched the Maryland Hall of Records. He found an ad for slaves being sold from that very slave ship. He even found the record of sale of Kunta Kinte. The story was now complete.

In 1976, Haley finished his epic book *Roots*. It had taken him 12 years to write. The book was a huge success. Within a year, it had sold 8 million copies. *Roots* was made into a 12-hour television miniseries. More people watched *Roots* than any other show that had come before it.

In April 1977, Haley won a Pulitzer Prize for *Roots*. He was busy with book signings and lectures. This left little time for more writing.

Finally, in the late 1980s, Haley began a book called *Queen*. It was to be the story of his father's side of the family from 1882 to 1967. He never finished this book. On February 10, 1992, he died of a heart attack.

Another writer finished *Queen*. It was published in 1993. It was later made into a six-hour miniseries. Also after Haley's death, the movie *Malcolm X* was released. It was based on Haley's original book.

Alex Haley's two books had a huge impact. *Roots* told of a lost part of American history. It was the story of the Africans brought to America to be slaves. *The Autobiography of Malcolm X* helped Americans understand a man who was a key part of the struggle for civil rights. Because of Haley's work, America's story is better understood.

Alex Haley said the Coast Guard played an important role in his success. He said the service taught him discipline and a good work ethic. In 1973, the Coast Guard gave him its Distinguished Public Service Award. In 1989, he received an honorary degree from the U.S. Coast Guard Academy. He was the first person in history to be so honored. In 1999, the ship U.S.C.G.C. *Alex Haley* was named for Haley. The ship's emblem includes Haley's personal motto: "Find the Good and Praise It."

In 2002, the Kunta Kinte-Alex Haley Memorial was dedicated in Annapolis, Maryland. The Memorial includes a statue of Alex Haley. He is reading a book to three children of different ethnic backgrounds. The book he holds is the story of Kunta Kinte's arrival in America.

According to its Web site, the Memorial portrays "Alex Haley's vision for racial (harmony) and healing. (It) symbolizes in Kunta Kinte and his descendants the triumph of the human spirit in very difficult times."

Remembering the Facts

1. How did Alex learn his family history as a child?

2. How did Haley pass the time on long sea voyages?

3. What was Haley's first success in selling a story?

4. What kind of writing did Haley do as Chief Journalist?

5. What work did Haley do for *Reader's Digest*?

6. What new style of interview did Haley become known for?

7. Why was Haley's idea to write his family history unique?

8. How did Haley finally learn the story of Kunta Kinte?

Understanding the Story

9. Why do you think *Roots* was important in America's history?

10. How do you think Haley's grandmother was like the African storytellers?

Getting the Main Idea

In what ways do you think Alex Haley is a good role model for young Americans?

Applying What You've Learned

Make a poster that shows your family tree, or write a report about your background.

Muhammad Ali

Boxer

Muhammad Ali is one of the most exciting sports stars in history. He is a three-time heavyweight boxing champion of the world. Ali says that boxing is only a small part of who he is. After he retired from boxing, Ali began what he calls his "true work." This was his fight against injustice and poverty around the world.

Muhammad Ali was born on January 17, 1942, in Louisville, Kentucky. His parents named him Cassius Marcellus Clay Jr. (He changed his name as an adult.) Cassius was the older of two boys. His mother cleaned houses and worked as a cook. His father was a sign painter. He also painted billboards and murals.

Cassius's parents gave him strong values. He learned that prejudice was wrong. He learned to treat others with respect. He learned to be dignified in the face of injustice.

The family had little money. Their house was small and in poor condition. They bought their clothing at second-hand stores. The boys had bicycles to ride to school. Cassius treasured his shiny, red bike.

One day, Cassius and a friend rode their bikes to the fair. Cassius's bike was stolen. He wanted to report the crime. He found a policeman in a nearby gym. He found something else in the gym, too. Everywhere he looked, he saw boxers in training. Cassius knew right away that he wanted to learn how to box. After his parents agreed, he began training.

Cassius Clay was 13 years old. He weighed 85 pounds. He had a lot of endurance. He won fights by wearing the other boxer out. Soon he was appearing in boxing matches on a local TV show. He earned $4 for each fight. This was a lot to a boy in 1955.

Cassius decided he was going to be the heavyweight champion of the world. He set up a strict schedule to help him reach his goal. Every day he went to school from 8 A.M. to 2 P.M. He worked in the library from 2 P.M. to 6 P.M. to earn money. After that, he trained from 6 P.M. to midnight.

Cassius began to develop his own style. He punched with lightning speed. He moved around the ring quickly to avoid his opponent. He also developed his trademark skill. He would throw a quick punch. Then he would lean back fast. His opponent's punch would miss him.

Cassius grew in size and strength. By the time he was 16, he was 6 feet tall and 170 pounds. In both 1959 and 1960, he won the national Golden Gloves title. In 1960, he made the U.S. Olympic boxing team as a light heavyweight.

The Olympics were held in Rome, Italy. Cassius Clay won fight after fight. In the end, he won the Olympic gold medal. Millions of people watched Clay fight on television. They cheered for the handsome young man from Kentucky.

Clay returned home to Louisville to a hero's welcome. He was honored by the governor and the mayor. He was even given a parade down the main street. After the parade, he went into a restaurant to eat. But the restaurant refused to serve him because he was black. Clay was so angry, he threw his gold medal into the Ohio River.

He later said, "I had won the gold medal for America. But I still couldn't eat in this restaurant in my hometown. The town where they all knew my name… where I went to church and led a Christian life.… I had won the gold medal. But it didn't mean anything, because I didn't have the right skin color."

Clay turned professional. He chose Angelo Dundee as his trainer. Dundee had trained many famous fighters. Clay trained hard. Dundee said, "Clay was always the first in and the last out of the gym!"

On February 25, 1964, Clay had the biggest fight of his career. He fought Sonny Liston for the heavyweight title. Clay won the fight in the seventh round. At 22, Clay had met his goal. He was the new heavyweight champion of the world.

Cassius Clay loved to talk about himself. He went on and on about how great he was. He wrote silly, boastful poems about himself. He would shout, "I am beautiful. I am the greatest. I can't be beat. I'm the fastest thing on two feet. I float like a butterfly and sting like a bee." All this attracted a lot of attention. Clay was becoming a star as well as a famous boxer.

In 1963, Clay joined a religious group called the Nation of Islam. Members of this group are Muslims. He chose a new name: Muhammad Ali.

In the 1960s, the Nation of Islam believed that blacks should form their own country. They felt this was the only way blacks would ever be treated fairly. Ali was tired of racism. He felt that being a member of the Nation of Islam would be a good way to fight for civil rights for blacks.

Many people feared the Nation of Islam. Ali was criticized by both blacks and whites. He even received death threats. Ali stayed true to his new Muslim faith. In 1975, he left the Nation of Islam sect to become a Sunni Muslim. This group taught that all men were brothers.

Ali was about to face a bigger fight than any he had fought in the ring. In 1964, the United States entered the Vietnam War. Many Americans believed that the country should not have been in this war. Even so, thousands of young men were drafted to serve in the military. If a man was drafted, it was against the law for him not to serve.

In 1967, Muhammad Ali was drafted. He refused to serve. He said war was against his religious beliefs. He was sentenced to five years in jail. He was fined $10,000. His lawyers appealed. Soon he was free on bail.

The worst was yet to come. Ali's boxing licenses were taken away. The World Boxing Association took away his world heavyweight title. Ali was unable to box in the United States. Next, the government took away his passport. This meant he could no longer box overseas. It would be three years before he could fight again.

Ali had no way of earning a living. He had huge expenses. He had a wife and children. He also had several lawyers to pay.

Ali began speaking at colleges to raise money. He was surprised to learn that he was a hero to many students. They agreed with him that the Vietnam War was wrong. Ali told the students, "I would like to say to those of you who think I've lost so much, I have gained everything. I have peace of heart. I have a clear, free conscience. And I'm proud!"

Ali did other things to earn money. He appeared on TV talk shows. He signed a book deal for his life story. It was called *The Greatest: My Own Story*. He even appeared in a Broadway play.

Ali was winning a great deal of public support. At the same time, the war was becoming less popular. Finally, on June 20, 1970, his suspension from boxing was lifted. In October of that year, he returned to the ring. He won a fight against Jerry Quarry in three rounds.

Ali then won a more important fight. On June 28, 1971, the U.S. Supreme Court ruled in Ali's favor. He was found not guilty of draft evasion. The judges believed that war really was against Ali's religion. Now he could go on with his career.

Ali was 29 years old. He had been out of boxing for three years. He was determined to regain his heavyweight title. To do this, he would have to beat Joe Frazier. Frazier had become the heavyweight champion while Ali was suspended. The two met on March 8, 1971. The match was called "The Fight of the Century."

In the 11th round, Frazier won the fight. Ali vowed they would fight again. On January 28, 1974, the two did meet again. This time Ali won. Ali did not regain his title, though. Frazier had lost it in the meantime to George Foreman.

Ali fought George Foreman in Zaire, Africa. The fight was called "The Rumble in the Jungle." Ali won. Now he was the heavyweight champion of the world for a second time.

On February 15, 1978, Ali was beaten by Leon Spinks. A few months later, he beat Spinks in a re-match. Ali was the heavyweight champion of the world for the third time. No other boxer in history had matched this feat. On June 27, 1979, Ali retired from boxing.

Ali found a new direction for his life. He used his fame and wealth to fight injustice and poverty. He spread a message of peace. He worked to help the poor.

Ali said, "When you saw me in the boxing ring fighting, it wasn't just so I could beat my opponent. My fighting had a purpose. I had to be successful in order to get people to listen to the things I had to say. I wanted to go to the people, where unemployment, drugs, and poverty were part of everyday life.... I hoped to inspire others to take control of their lives and to live with pride and self-determination."

In 1984, Ali was diagnosed with Parkinson's disease. This disease causes tremors (shaking). It causes poor balance and difficulty in speaking. Today Ali cannot speak easily. His mind is still active and sharp.

In 1996, Ali was honored for being an outstanding athlete and humanitarian. He was chosen to light the flame to start the Olympic Games in Atlanta. He slowly moved into the spotlight. As he lifted the torch, his arms shook. The huge crowd cheered for their hero.

Ali was named a U.N. Messenger of Peace in 1998. He traveled often to Africa and Asia. There he talked about human rights. He talked about tolerance and respect for others.

The Muhammad Ali Center in Louisville opened in 2005. It is a showcase for the values that are important to Ali. He hopes it will help people of all faiths to get along better.

In *The Greatest,* Ali says, "I would like to be remembered as a man who won the heavyweight title three times, who was humorous, and who treated everyone right. As a man who never looked down on those who looked up to him, and who helped as many people as he could. As a man who stood up for his beliefs no matter what. As a man who tried to unite all humankind through faith and love. And if that's too much, then I guess I'd settle for being remembered only as a great boxer who became a leader and a champion of his people. And I wouldn't even mind if folks forget how pretty I was."

Remembering the Facts

1. How did a stolen bike lead Cassius Clay to boxing?

2. What was Cassius's trademark skill as a boxer?

3. What honor did Cassius Clay win in 1960?

4. What was the result of Clay's beating Sonny Liston?

5. Why did Cassius Clay change his name to Muhammad Ali?

6. Why couldn't Ali box for three years in the 1960s?

7. How did Ali use his fame after he retired from boxing?

8. How would Ali like to be remembered?

Understanding the Story

9. Why do you think Muhammad Ali was chosen to light the Olympic flame?

10. Many people looked down on Ali when he refused to serve in the military. Why do you think the public supported Ali in the end?

Getting the Main Idea

Why do you think Muhammad Ali is a champion both in and out of the boxing ring?

Applying What You've Learned

Muhammad Ali became known for his silly, boastful poems about himself. Write a short poem about yourself using his style.

Faith Ringgold
Artist

Faith Ringgold is an important American artist. She is best known for her beautiful story quilts. Her quilts combine painting, quilting, and storytelling. They hang in major museums around the world.

Ringgold is also a children's book author. *Tar Beach* was a Caldecott Honor Book. It won the Coretta Scott King Illustrator Award. Since 1991, she has written and illustrated more than 17 children's books.

Faith Ringgold was born on October 8, 1930, in New York City. She was the youngest of three children. The family lived on the fourth floor of an apartment building in Harlem. Faith's father was a garbage truck driver. Before Faith was three, her parents split up. She was raised by her mother.

Faith began having asthma attacks when she was two years old. The attacks often put her in the hospital. Because of her health, Faith didn't go to school until second grade.

Later, Faith said that having asthma was "perfect for making art." She would spend hours at home. She would draw quietly. She would make things from bits of cloth. She always had some kind of art project going.

When Faith felt well, her mother took her to art museums. Sometimes they went to see a show on Broadway. On other days they went to Harlem's Apollo Theater. Faith saw Louis Armstrong, Duke Ellington, Frank Sinatra, and many other well-known performers.

Harlem was a poor but tight-knit neighborhood. There was very little crime. No one locked their doors. Everyone in the neighborhood looked out for one another. Nobody had telephones. Children ran messages for their parents. They also went to the store to shop for their parents.

In those days, families typically gathered around the radio. The TV had been invented, but very few people owned one. They listened to programs like *The Shadow, Amos 'n' Andy*, and *The Jack Benny Show*. Listeners used their imaginations to picture the action.

On hot summer nights, Faith's family went up to the roof of the building. There they hoped to catch the breeze. They called the tar-covered roof "Tar Beach." The family would picnic on the roof. The adults played cards or talked. The children lay on the blankets and looked at the stars. They had a lot of fun.

Faith's mother taught her the importance of education. Faith loved learning. But she didn't like going to school. She never had a black teacher in all her years in school. She remembers some of her white teachers making fun of their black students.

In 1942, when Faith was 12, her family moved to the Sugar Hill section of Harlem. Sugar Hill got its name because of the "sweet" lifestyle of the people who lived there. Some of its famous residents were Thurgood Marshall, W. E. B. DuBois, Mary McLeod Bethune, Duke Ellington, and heavyweight champion Joe Louis.

Faith's mother took a job in a defense plant. She sewed jackets for the army. She also made clothes for friends and family. In the late 1940s, she went to the Fashion Institute of Technology. There she honed her sewing and designing skills. This was the start of Faith's mother's career in fashion design.

In June 1949, Faith graduated from high school. She went on to nearby City College. Faith wanted to major in art. At the time, only men could be art majors in the School of Liberal Arts. Faith had to take classes at the School of Education. There she studied art education.

Faith planned to be an artist. Her teachers tried to discourage her. One teacher even laughed at her. He told her she couldn't draw.

Years later, Faith was awarded an honorary doctorate in fine art from City College. In her acceptance speech she said, "The harder you work, the more talented you will become. Your talent can only be defined by you."

In 1950, at age 20, Faith married Earl Wallace. He was a classical and jazz pianist. The couple had two daughters, Michele and Barbara. Soon Earl began abusing drugs. The couple divorced.

In 1955, Faith graduated from City College with a B.S. in Fine Art and Education. She taught art in the public schools for the next 18 years. In 1959, she completed her M.A. in art at City College.

In 1961, she took her mother and daughters to Europe. There she studied the work of the masters. When she returned home, she began painting seriously. In 1962, Faith married Burdette "Birdie" Ringgold.

The summer of 1963 was the beginning of Faith's mature work as a painter. She had read the works of James Baldwin. He wrote about problems between blacks and whites. She had heard Dr. Martin Luther King Jr. speak. She wanted to make her own statement about the civil rights movement. She would do this using her art.

Ringgold hoped to make the fight for civil rights "super real" to everyone. She called her new style "Super Realism." In this style, she did a series of more than 20 oil paintings. She called it her American People Series. The paintings showed the civil rights movement from the viewpoint of a black woman.

In 1966, Ringgold had her first art gallery show. She was part of a group show called "Art of the American Negro." It was the first black art exhibition in Harlem since the 1930s. That same year, she joined the Spectrum Gallery. About 20 painters and sculptors were in the group. Ringgold was the only black artist.

Her first one-person art show at the Spectrum Gallery was in 1967. It was titled "American People." For the show, Ringgold painted three large murals. *The Flag Is Bleeding* showed a white woman acting as peacemaker between a black man and a white man. *U.S. Postage Stamp Commemorating the Advent of Black Power* showed 100 black and white faces. *Die* was inspired by the deaths of Malcolm X and Robert Kennedy. The show also featured the smaller paintings from Ringgold's American People Series.

The show was a success. Ringgold got good reviews in art publications. She also sold two paintings.

Ringgold did some fund-raising work for the Southern Christian Leadership Conference (SCLC). The SCLC asked civil-rights activist Fannie Lou Hamer to speak at a fashion show. The event was run by Ringgold's mother. Hamer's lecture convinced Ringgold to help make changes for black Americans.

In 1970, Ringgold had her second one-person show at the Spectrum Gallery. It was called "American Black." The 12 paintings in this show were called her Black Light Series.

In 1973, Ringgold resigned from teaching. She wanted to make art her full-time job. She began to lecture and go on traveling exhibitions at colleges. Between 1969 and 2006, she worked in printmaking, painting, soft sculpture, doll making, cloth masks, quilts, and performance art.

Throughout the 1970s, Ringgold worked more and more with fabric. She began to sew fabric borders around her paintings. She had seen this done in Tibetan paintings.

In 1980, Ringgold created her first painted quilt, *Echoes of Harlem*. It was the only quilt she worked on with her mother. Ringgold painted 30 portraits of Harlem residents. This formed the center of the quilt. The portraits were joined together with quilted fabric.

Soon after the quilt was finished, Ringgold's mother died. Ringgold decided she would make at least one quilt each year in her mother's memory. To date, she has made more than 75. One work, called *Mother's Quilt* (1983), has nine doll shapes. The dolls represent a mother and eight daughters.

Back in 1979, Ringgold wrote her autobiography. She never found anyone to publish it. She looked for other ways to publish her writing. She began writing her stories on her quilts. This was the beginning of her work with story quilts.

Her first story quilt was *Who's Afraid of Aunt Jemima?* (1983). Each quilt section acts as a "page." The story is written in parts on the sections. A person looking at the quilt reads the story standing up. The stories must be brief and quick-moving.

Ringgold continued doing story quilts. Her best-known story quilt is *Tar Beach* (1988). The quilt tells the story of eight-year-old Cassie. Her family takes her up to the roof on hot summer nights. Cassie dreams that she can make her family's problems all go away. She dreams she can fly over buildings. At the end of the story, Cassie says, "Anyone can fly. All you have to do is have somewhere to go that you can't get to any other way. The next thing you know you're flying among the stars."

A children's book editor saw the *Tar Beach* story quilt. She read the story on the quilt. She knew right away it would make a good children's book. The book was published in 1991. It won a Caldecott Honor award for its artwork. It also won the Coretta Scott King Illustrator Award. The winner's work must "promote understanding and appreciation of the culture of all peoples and their contribution to the realization of the American dream." *Tar Beach* also won the *New York Times* award for the best children's book of 1991. Faith Ringgold began a new career as a children's book author. She has written and illustrated more than 17 children's books.

Ringgold was a professor of art at the University of California at San Diego from 1984 to 2002. She is the founder of the Anyone Can Fly Foundation. This group works to introduce black artists to kids and adults.

Ringgold says, "My ideas come from reflecting on my life and the lives of people I have known and have been in some way inspired by.… Writing children's books has provided me with a perfect vehicle to communicate my ideas and vision and, I hope, give back to children some of the magic they have shown me." Her motto on her Web site is "If One Can, Anyone Can. All You Gotta Do Is Try."

Remembering the Facts

1. Why did Faith do many art projects as a child?

2. What was the tar beach?

3. How did Faith's mother get her start in fashion design?

4. What was the subject of Ringgold's American People Series?

5. What is a story quilt?

6. What is Ringgold's best-known story quilt?

7. How did Ringgold get her start writing books for children?

8. What is the purpose of the Anyone Can Fly Foundation?

Understanding the Story

9. Why do you think few American art museums prior to 1970 showed works by African Americans or women?

10. Quilts serve many purposes besides providing warmth. They save memories. They tell stories. How do you think Faith Ringgold's quilts fit into this tradition?

Getting the Main Idea

In what ways do you think Faith Ringgold is a good role model for young Americans?

Applying What You've Learned

Design a story quilt of your own on a sheet of paper. It should include drawings or designs and a written story.

Alice Walker
Author

Alice Walker is more than just an author. She is a civil rights activist. She also was one of the first college professors to teach about black female authors. Her most famous book is *The Color Purple*. She won the Pulitzer Prize for this book in 1983. The book was made into a movie that was nominated for 11 Academy Awards. It was also a long-running Broadway play.

Alice was born on February 9, 1944, in Eatonton, Georgia. Her parents were sharecroppers. Sharecroppers farmed another person's land for a share of the crop earnings. Half the money went to the land owner. The Walker family kept the other half.

The Walker family lived in a tiny house in the country. Alice was the youngest of eight children. All the children worked hard in the fields. For their work, the family earned about $300 a year.

Alice was a bright student. She liked to perform and speak at church. She was also an active girl. She especially liked playing outside.

One day when she was eight, she was playing with her brothers. By mistake, one of them shot Alice in the eye with a BB gun. The eye developed a large white scar. She could no longer see out of that eye.

The children at school teased her about her eye. Alice became quiet and sad. She kept to herself. She read a lot. She also wrote poetry.

When Alice was 14, doctors removed the white scar from her eye. Her eye looked normal again. But Alice never got her sight back in that eye.

Alice did well in high school. She graduated at the top of her class. She was elected prom queen. She won a scholarship to Spelman College in Atlanta. Spelman was the best school in the country for black women.

Alice's mother was proud of her daughter. Somehow, she saved money from her small earnings to buy Alice three gifts. These were a suitcase, a sewing machine, and a typewriter. The suitcase stood for independence. The sewing machine meant self-sufficiency. The typewriter was a tool for creativity.

Alice arrived at Spelman in the fall of 1961. At this time, the civil rights movement was just beginning. Students across the South joined the movement. Alice took part in protests and rallies.

At the same time, Alice worked hard at her studies. She took many classes in literature. She loved reading the works of Tolstoy. He was a Russian writer from the 19th century. Tolstoy described his characters so well that Alice felt she knew them. His love for his native land was also clear in his work. Alice used Tolstoy as a model for her own work.

At the end of her freshman year, Alice was chosen for a great honor. She was asked to be a delegate to the Youth World Peace Festival in Helsinki, Finland. As a delegate, she was invited to the home of Dr. Martin Luther King Jr. and his wife, Coretta. The Kings wanted to meet the students going to the festival. At the Peace Festival, Alice learned that the struggle for peace was worldwide.

The next summer, Alice went to Washington, D.C. On August 28, 1963, she joined the famous March on Washington for Jobs and Freedom. She heard Dr. King give his "I Have a Dream" speech.

She would never forget that day. She said, "It was one of those days when you feel the tide is turning and you are with the tide. I heard every word, and every word went through my whole body and through my whole soul."

In the fall, Alice was offered a scholarship to Sarah Lawrence College. She would study literature. The college was far away in Bronxville, New York. Alice left Spelman and headed for New York.

Alice soon found that this college in New York was very different from the all-black school she went to in the South. There were just three black students at Sarah Lawrence. Many of the students were from wealthy homes. It was a huge change for her.

During her senior year, Alice became depressed. She thought about ending her life. She began to write many poems and stories. At last, she worked through her problem. She realized how much she loved life.

In 1965, Alice wrote one of her first short stories, "To Hell with Dying." The story is about family, love, and memories. Langston Hughes, a famous black poet, read the story. Impressed, he included the story in a 1967 book. It was called *The Best Short Stories of Negro Writers.*

Alice graduated from college in 1965. She returned to the South. She began to work in the voter registration drive. At that time, many white people in the South did not want blacks to vote. Civil rights workers went door to door in black neighborhoods. They helped people register to vote.

While Walker was doing this work, she met Mel Leventhal. He was a young white Jewish law student. He was also a volunteer in the civil rights movement. They were later married and had one daughter.

At the end of the summer, the two returned to New York City. Mel attended law school. Alice began writing full time.

She wrote an essay called "The Civil Rights Movement: What Good Was It?" In it she told about her experiences in the civil rights movement. She said, "The civil rights movement gave us history and men far greater than Presidents. It gave us heroes, selfless men of courage and strength, for our little boys and girls to follow. It called us to life. Because we live, it can never die."

For this essay, she won a $300 first prize in *American Scholar's* annual essay contest. The essay was her first published article.

In 1967, Walker and Leventhal moved to Jackson, Mississippi. Leventhal worked on civil rights cases for the NAACP. Walker was a black history consultant to a Head Start program. She began writing a novel. Their life in Jackson was not easy. Because they were a mixed-race couple, they received many threats.

In 1968, Alice Walker became writer-in-residence at Jackson State University. While there, she published a book of poetry called *Once*. She also wrote her first novel, *The Third Life of Grange Copeland*. A few days after she finished the book, her daughter Rebecca was born.

The Third Life of Grange Copeland got good reviews. In 1970, Walker was appointed writer-in-residence at Tougaloo College in Jackson. Then in 1972, she was offered a teaching job at Wellesley College in Massachusetts. So Walker left the South.

At Wellesley, Walker taught a class in women's studies. She centered the course on the writings of black women. Today most colleges offer such courses. Walker's course was one of the first in the country.

While she was preparing her course, Walker discovered the work of Zora Neale Hurston. Hurston, a black writer, had been well-known during the 1920s. By the early 1970s, her books were out of print and forgotten. One of Hurston's books that Walker loved best was *Their Eyes Were Watching God*. Walker worked to bring popular attention to Hurston's writing.

Later Walker learned that Hurston had died alone in a nursing home in Florida. She had been buried in an unmarked grave. Walker went to Florida. She cleaned up the grave site. She had a headstone placed at the grave.

Walker continued her own writing. *In Love and Trouble: Stories of Black Women* is a collection of short stories. *Revolutionary Petunias and Other Poems* is a book of poetry. In 1974, she published *Langston*

Hughes, American Poet. She wanted to honor Hughes for the help he gave her early in her career. Walker's second novel, *Meridian,* was published in 1976.

Alice Walker and Mel Leventhal were divorced in 1977. Walker moved to San Francisco to get a fresh start. She became a professor at the University of California at Berkeley.

In 1982, Alice Walker published *The Color Purple.* The book takes place in Georgia during the early- to mid-1900s. It tells the story of a young black girl, Celie Harris. Celie is a poor, uneducated, and abused child.

When she grows up, Celie is able to overcome her past. Through love she is able to become independent and confident. She is able to find her unique voice in the world. *The Color Purple* is a story of hope. It is a story of the healing power of love. It is a book that celebrates life.

The book was a hit. *Newsweek* called it "an American novel of permanent importance." *Essence* called it "one of the great books of our time." *The Color Purple* was awarded the Pulitzer Prize in 1983. Walker also received an American Book Award.

The Color Purple was made into a movie. Steven Spielberg was the director. The stars were Whoopi Goldberg, Margaret Avery, Oprah Winfrey, and Danny Glover. The movie received 11 Academy Award nominations.

Walker's sister Ruth started the Color Purple Foundation in her sister's honor. This group has given scholarships to needy students. It also funds summer programs for inner-city youth.

The Color Purple was made into a Broadway play. It ran for more than two years, ending in February 2008. There were 910 performances.

Alice Walker has written many other books. As of this writing, she has written 15 novels and books of short stories. She has written eight books of poetry and 11 non-fiction books. She continues to speak out about today's issues.

Remembering the Facts

1. What kind of work did Alice Walker's parents do?

2. How did Alice lose her vision in one eye?

3. How was Walker affected by Dr. Martin Luther King Jr.'s "I Have a Dream" speech?

4. How did Langston Hughes help Walker's career?

5. In what way was Walker's course on women's studies unusual?

6. Why did Walker and her husband receive threats while living in Jackson, Mississippi?

7. For which novel did Walker win the Pulitzer Prize?

8. What is the purpose of the Color Purple Foundation?

Understanding the Story

9. How do you think Alice Walker's mother likely influenced Alice's creative spirit?

10. How did the civil rights movement influence Alice Walker?

Getting the Main Idea

In what ways do you think Alice Walker is a good role model for today's youth?

Applying What You've Learned

Alice Walker said the following when she heard Dr. Martin Luther King Jr. speak: "I heard every word, and every word went through my whole body and my whole soul."

Write a paragraph describing a time when you heard a speaker who made you feel this way.

Gladys Knight

Singer

Millions of Americans watch the TV show *American Idol*. Singers compete for votes on the show. The audience eagerly waits to see who will win. The winning singer gets a huge career boost.

Years ago, Ted Mack's *The Original Amateur Hour* worked in much the same way. It aired on TV for 23 years. Many famous singers of the past got their start on this show. Frank Sinatra, Pat Boone, Ann-Margret, and Maria Callas all appeared on the *The Original Amateur Hour*.

In 1951, Gladys Knight won the grand prize on the *The Original Amateur Hour*. She was only seven years old. The tiny first-grader couldn't reach the microphone. She had to stand on a box to sing. When she sang Nat King Cole's "Too Young," she brought down the house. Tiny Gladys had a big, big voice! She went on to become one of the most famous singers of all time.

Gladys Knight was born on May 28, 1944, in Atlanta, Georgia. She learned to love education, the church, and gospel music. Gladys grew up in a house full of music. Both of her parents were singers in a gospel choir.

Gladys has said that she's been singing for as long as she could breathe. At age four, she sang solos in the Mount Mariah Baptist Church. At five, she was performing with the Morris Brown College Choir in Atlanta. At seven, she won the *The Original Amateur Hour*. At eight, she and some of her family members formed a singing group. The group included Gladys, her brother Merald ("Bubba"), her sister Brenda, and cousins William and Eleanor Guest.

The children practiced on Wednesday nights after choir practice. An older cousin, James Woods, became their "manager." James's nickname was Pip. The group practiced their songs at Pip's house. They also learned dance steps. They didn't want to look boring by standing still as they sang.

Pip booked their first performance. It was at a ladies' club meeting at the YMCA. After that, the group had many gigs. They sang at parties, reunions, and fish fries.

After a few months, Pip entered the group in a talent contest. The contest was at the El Morocco Lounge in Atlanta. First prize was a two-week contract to sing at the Royal Peacock. This was one of the hottest clubs on the Chitlin' Circuit. The Chitlin' Circuit was the nickname for the string of venues that were safe for black entertainers to perform in during the time of racial segregation. The top acts in jazz and rhythm and blues (R&B) all performed at the Royal Peacock.

There was one problem. The group didn't have a name. They had to decide on a name before they could sing in the contest. They took the nickname of their manager. They became The Pips.

The contest went on for three weeks. In the end, The Pips won. Their winning song was "To Be Loved."

Ten-year-old Gladys and The Pips put on two shows a night at the Royal Peacock. The pay was only $10 a night. Still, they were making a name for themselves. Soon they were performing all over the Southeast.

In the summer of 1955, The Pips began working with Maurice King. King helped the group develop their voices. He helped them work on their harmony.

King found a new song called "Whistle My Love." He arranged for The Pips to record it with Brunswick Records. The record did not sell well. Gladys's sister Brenda and cousin Eleanor left the group. The two were replaced by cousins Edward Patten and Langston George.

When Gladys was 12, she and The Pips went on a road tour. The tour included some of the top stars of Brunswick Records. The Pips toured with Jackie Wilson and Sam Cooke. The stars treated The Pips well. Life on the road was not easy for black artists prior to the civil rights movement.

Blacks were discriminated against. Blacks were not welcome in most hotels. Boarding houses owned by blacks provided places to stay. Blacks had to go to the back door of restaurants to be served. One time, The Pips tried to rent a hotel room in Little Rock, Arkansas. Policemen pressured them to get out of town.

When Gladys was in eighth grade, her father left the family. Her mother had to work two jobs to make ends meet. Life was hard. Gladys later said, "We survived by laughing at those things that were laughable. We prayed for those that were not.… We were poor in goods but rich in spirit."

During these hard times, Gladys took refuge in school and music. She was on the track team and the yearbook staff. She sang in the choir, and she was a cheerleader.

Gladys's 16th year, 1961, was a year of firsts. She graduated from high school. She and The Pips recorded their first record. The group had their first song on the charts.

The Pips recorded "Every Beat of My Heart" with Fury Records in 1961. Gladys was the lead singer on the song. It was released as Gladys Knight and the Pips. The song hit #1 on the R&B chart. Soon after, Langston George left the group.

In 1962, Gladys Knight and the Pips recorded their first full album on Fury Records. Two of the songs made the Top Five on the charts. Knight and the Pips were still making very little money. They kept on working.

Gladys had already married by age 16. She had two children by the age of 18. (A third was born later.) Gladys did not slow down. The family moved to New York City. Gladys resumed her singing career.

Gladys's husband began using drugs. He left his family. Knight was just 20 years old with two young children to raise. Her mother helped by keeping the children when Knight went on the road for singing tours.

Gladys's mother gave Gladys a necklace with a mustard seed on it. Gladys's mother was a Christian. She said the necklace was symbolic of a passage in the Bible. It says if you have as much faith as would fit on a mustard seed, you will be able to move mountains.

Gladys's mother also taught Knight and the Pips how to do a prayer chain. They would join hands. They said a prayer before performing.

In 1966, Gladys Knight and the Pips got a gig at the Apollo Theater in New York. This is a famous theater. It is in the historically black Harlem neighborhood. All the greats played there. A few of these singers were Nat King Cole, Ella Fitzgerald, Count Basie, and Miles Davis. Berry Gordy, founder of Motown Records, saw Knight and the Pips perform. He was impressed. He convinced them to sign a recording contract.

At the time, Motown only recorded black artists. It played an important role in the racial integration of popular music. The first song Knight and the Pips recorded for Motown was "I Heard It Through the Grapevine" in 1967. The song rocketed to #1 on the R&B chart. It stayed there six weeks.

Another big hit was "Neither One of Us (Wants to Be the First to Say Goodbye)." Knight and the Pips won their first Grammy for this song.

Gladys Knight and the Pips signed a contract with Buddah Records in 1973. It was a good fit. Their career took off. Their first album with Buddah was *Imagination*. The album not only went gold, it had three gold singles. One of these was "Midnight Train to Georgia." This song was their first #1 hit on the pop chart. In 1974, they won Grammys in both the R&B and the Pop categories.

Legal problems meant Knight and the Pips could not record together in the last half of the 1970s. Things worked out. They were back together in 1980.

In 1985, Knight recorded "That's What Friends Are For" with Elton John, Dionne Warwick, and Stevie Wonder. This was a benefit recording for the American Foundation for AIDS Research. It held the #1 R&B spot and the #13 pop spot for four weeks. In 1988, "Love Overboard" was a #1 R&B hit for Gladys Knight and the Pips. It also won a Grammy.

In 1988, Gladys Knight left the Pips to follow a solo career. She continued to perform hits from the Pips days. She also added new music. Knight sang soul, gospel, and pop with great feeling and energy.

In all, Gladys Knight has recorded more than 38 albums. She and the Pips produced some of the most popular songs of the 1960s, 1970s, and 1980s. In 1995, Knight got her star on the Hollywood Walk of Fame. Gladys Knight and the Pips were inducted into the Rock and Roll Hall of Fame in 1996.

In 1997, Knight wrote her autobiography, *Between Each Line of Pain and Glory*. She and the Pips were also presented with Lifetime Achievement awards from the Rhythm & Blues Hall of Fame and from BET (Black Entertainment Television).

Gladys Knight is still recording solo albums. She has made four albums in the last ten years. In 2002, her solo album *At Last* won a Grammy award. She performed the song "This Is Our Time" at the opening ceremonies of the 2002 Winter Olympics in Salt Lake City, Utah.

Knight sang a duet with Ray Charles on his album *Genius Loves Company*, released in 2005. They each won a Grammy for best gospel performance for their duet "Heaven Help Us."

In 2006, Knight released an album called *Before Me*. On this album, she honors singers who were her friends, mentors, and/or sources of inspiration to her over the years. All the profits from the album go to the Ashley Stewart Stores Community Foundation. This group works to improve the lives of children.

Gladys Knight is a national spokeswoman for the American Diabetes Association. Knight's mother died of diabetes in 1997. The family set up the Elizabeth Knight Foundation in her honor. It raises money to support diabetes research and awareness. This is important work, as more than 20 million Americans have diabetes.

Knight also wrote a book about healthy lifestyles. *At Home With Gladys Knight: Her Personal Recipe for Living Well, Eating Right, and Loving Life* was published in 2001. In it, she hopes to teach people how to make healthy choices to live longer and better. The book includes recipes, too.

Gladys Knight is one of the greatest singers of all time. She has been singing for more than half a century. She and the Pips stayed together nearly 40 years. They are one of the most respected soul groups.

Remembering the Facts

1. On what television show did Gladys Knight first gain fame?

2. How old was Gladys when she and family members formed The Pips?

3. What was the Chitlin' Circuit?

4. Why was life on the road not easy for black performers during the 1950s?

5. What was the first hit Gladys Knight and the Pips had for Motown Records?

6. What song was the group's first #1 pop hit?

7. What was the purpose of Knight's 2006 album *Before Me*?

8. Why did Knight write the book *At Home with Gladys Knight*?

Understanding the Story

9. Why do you think it is so difficult to become a recording artist?

10. How do you think Gladys Knight stayed true to the values she learned as a child?

Getting the Main Idea

In what ways do you think Gladys Knight is a good role model to young Americans?

Applying What You've Learned

Choose a subject about which you feel deeply. Write the words for a short song about this subject. Put your words to music if you'd like.

Bernice Johnson Reagon
Singer/Educator/Artist

For more than 40 years, Bernice Johnson Reagon has sung out for freedom and justice. Her voice is known to millions. She is known for her singing, composing, teaching, writing, and her museum exhibits.

Bernice Reagon founded Sweet Honey in the Rock. This is a female gospel singing group. For 30 years, Reagon sang with the group as its leader. She wrote songs for it. She directed and produced many of the group's recordings.

Reagon is also a historian and a teacher. She taught for years at American University in Washington, D.C. She is a curator emeritus at the Smithsonian's National Museum of American History.

Bernice Johnson was born on October 4, 1942, in Albany, Georgia. She was one of eight children. Her family was poor. Her mother was a housekeeper. During the summer, she worked in the cotton fields. She worked alongside her children. She used the money to buy school clothes for the next year. Bernice's father was a Baptist minister. To make ends meet, he also worked as a carpenter.

Bernice's parents were active in their community. Her father worked in voter registration drives. Her mother participated in church and school activities.

Bernice loved music. She sang in church. She sang in school. She sang on the playground. There was no piano in her school or church until she was 11 years old. Because of this, she sang a cappella (without instruments). Bernice learned spirituals and hymns. She became skilled at singing harmony. Bernice had a rich contralto voice. (Contralto means "the lowest female voice.")

Bernice also loved the blues. The blues were not allowed in the Johnson home. The children waited until their parents went to sleep. Then her brothers would listen to the blues on the radio in their room. Bernice and her sisters listened from their room through the wall. Bernice's favorite blues artist was Howlin' Wolf. She also loved B.B. King, Screamin' Jay Hawkins, and Muddy Waters.

In 1959, Bernice entered Albany State College. She majored in music. She planned a career singing classical music.

In 1961, the civil rights movement came to Albany. Meetings took place at the Mount Zion Baptist Church. People of all ages packed the church. One of the leaders was 18-year-old Cordell Reagon. He was a member of the Student Nonviolent Coordinating Committee (SNCC—pronounced "snick").

Bernice joined SNCC. She took part in marches. In November 1961, she and her best friend, Annette, were in the first mass march in Albany. Bernice joined in the protests. The administration at Albany State was afraid things would get out of hand. So, in 1961, school officials expelled the students who were seen as leaders of these activities. Bernice was one of them.

Cordell Reagon formed a singing group in 1962. He called it the SNCC Freedom Singers. Bernice joined the group. Bernice Johnson married Cordell. Later, the couple had two children. But they soon divorced. Bernice raised their children as a single parent.

Bernice Reagon spent the next five years as a Freedom Singer. The group toured the country to raise money. They worked for awareness of civil rights issues. Reagon loved telling the civil rights message in song. These years set the pattern for the rest of her life.

One of the people she met on her travels was activist Fannie Lou Hamer. They were both members of SNCC. The women often led songs together. At the 1964 Democratic convention in Atlantic City, New Jersey, Hamer and Reagon sang "Go Tell It on the Mountain." This was shown on national TV.

Bernice Reagon was inspired by Hamer. She called her a "fierce warrior" for the cause. Years later, Reagon wrote and recorded the song "Fannie Lou Hamer." She also made a tape of Hamer's singing. It was called "Songs My Mother Taught Me."

The SNCC Freedom Singers broke up the next year. Reagon began to organize folk festivals. She collected black songs and stories from the past. She started the Harambee Singers. This group sang civil rights music. The five women in the group dressed in African styles. They also wore their hair in natural afros. Reagon was one of the first women in SNCC to wear this style.

Bernice Reagon did a number of solo albums. Her first album was *Songs of the South*. It was released in 1964. She kept making solo albums even as her other work took off.

Reagon knew she needed more education to reach her goals. She decided to go to Spelman College. She earned a B.A. in history. She went to Howard University next. She earned a Ph.D. in history. Her doctoral thesis was called "The Songs of the Civil Rights Movement, 1955–1965: A Study in Culture History."

In 1972, the Smithsonian Institution decided to include exhibits on black history and culture in the museum. They asked Reagon to head a group to study black culture. Reagon traveled with a group of scholars. They went to Africa. They studied various cultural practices. They learned the roots of many modern traditions. When they got back, they created a festival program about what they had learned. Reagon's work was ground-breaking. Because of it, Reagon is known as one of the leading scholars in the field of black studies.

In 1973, Reagon formed a new singing group. The group was made up of five women. At their first practice, they sang the old song "Sweet Honey in the Rock." Reagon remembered singing this song as a child. Her father had told her the meaning of the song. It was about a land where, when rocks were cracked, honey would flow out of them. Reagon named the new group Sweet Honey in the Rock.

Sweet Honey in the Rock has celebrated more than 30 years together. Reagon retired from the group in 2004. Most often, the group has been made up of five singers.

The group sings spirituals and hymns. They also sing children's songs, blues, and jazz. They perform original pieces, too. Their sound has been based on five-part harmony. The songs have a message of justice, respect, and equality.

The group became very popular. Their first album, *Sweet Honey in the Rock*, was released in 1976. They won a Grammy Award for their 1988 version of singer Leadbelly's "Grey Goose."

In 1974, Reagon began working at the Smithsonian full time. She became director of the Program in African American Culture. She continued to study black culture. In 1988, she became a curator in the Smithsonian's Division of Home and Community Life. In 1989, she received a MacArthur Foundation "genius" grant to further her work.

One of Reagon's projects while at the Smithsonian was called *Wade in the Water*. This project, a series of radio programs, studied 19th- and 20th-century African-American sacred music. The programs showed the effect of sacred music on black history and culture. They showed how black history and culture also affected black sacred music.

Reagon spent 15 years researching the project. She spent another five years producing it. In 1994, this series of radio programs aired on National Public Radio. There were 26 one-hour programs in all.

For this work, Reagon won a Peabody Award. A traveling exhibit of *Wade in the Water* toured the country from 1996 to 2000. Reagon wrote a book on the same theme. It was called *We'll Understand It Better By and By: Pioneering African American Gospel Composers.*

In 1993, Reagon became a distinguished professor of history at American University in Washington, D.C. Also in 1993, she became a curator emeritus at the Smithsonian.

Reagon has won many awards. In 1995, she won the Charles Frankel Prize. This is awarded to a person who helps the public understand the humanities. The medal was presented to her at the White House by President Bill Clinton. In 1996, she won the Isadora Duncan Dance Award. This was for music she wrote for the ballet *Rock*. She also won a Heinz Award for the Arts and Humanities in 2003.

In 2001, she published *If You Don't Go, Don't Hinder Me—The African American Sacred Song Tradition.* Reagon says that sacred songs don't have to be church music. They can be other songs used in a sacred way. Some songs have a sacred purpose, such as those about the civil rights struggle.

Harriet Tubman and Sojourner Truth are Reagon's role models. She says the women were "singing…fighters whose lives taught me another way to be in this world." Both women fought injustice. Both used song to convey their message of human rights.

Bernice Reagon learned their lessons well. She has been a role model to millions of Americans. Her life work has been the telling of the African-American story. She has used her talents for singing, teaching, and historical research to help all Americans understand black history. And in doing so, she has helped everyone better understand America's story.

Remembering the Facts

1. Where did Bernice get her love of music?

2. How did Bernice learn to sing a cappella?

3. Why did Bernice get expelled from Albany State College?

4. How did Fannie Lou Hamer influence Reagon?

5. What was the subject of Reagon's Ph.D. work?

6. What is the message in the songs of Sweet Honey in the Rock?

7. What was the theme of the *Wade in the Water* series of radio programs?

8. What was the purpose of Reagon's African-American exhibit at the Smithsonian?

Understanding the Story

9. Why do you think Reagon chose Harriet Tubman and Sojourner Truth as role models?

10. Reagon said Sweet Honey in the Rock is a good symbol for black women. Explain what you think she meant.

Getting the Main Idea

In what ways do you think Bernice Reagon is a good role model for young Americans?

Applying What You've Learned

Bernice Reagon is a historian as well as a scholar and musician. Think of an everyday item or event. It could be as simple as a school dance. Research the history of that item or event and its impact on culture today.

Colin Powell
Statesman/Soldier

Colin Powell was a soldier for 35 years. He was a four-star general. He was the first African-American chairman of the Joint Chiefs of Staff. He was also the first African-American U.S. Secretary of State.

Powell is a respected problem-solver. His ideas are both fair and insightful. Presidents Reagan, George H. W. Bush, Clinton, and George W. Bush have all looked to him for advice. Powell has served his country for most of his adult life.

Colin Luther Powell was born on April 5, 1937, in New York City. His parents were from Jamaica. They had moved to New York City in the 1920s. They settled in the Harlem neighborhood. Neither had finished high school. His father was a shipping clerk. His mother was a seamstress. Colin had one older sister, Marilyn.

When Colin was three years old, the family left Harlem for the Bronx. The Bronx was a working-class New York City neighborhood. Many ethnic groups lived there. Irish, Italians, Puerto Ricans, blacks, and Polish all lived side by side. Colin learned to get along with different people.

Colin's parents taught their children to work hard. They told them, "Strive for a good education. Make something of your life."

Colin did not listen to this advice. He made little effort in school. His grades were low. He was placed in a special needs class in fifth grade. Colin's interests were playing stickball and riding his bicycle.

Colin graduated from high school in 1954. He had a C average. Still, his parents made it clear that they wanted him to go to college. So Colin went to City College of New York. Anyone who had graduated from a New York City high school could go there for a $10 fee.

City College had an Army Reserve Officers' Training Corps (ROTC) program. Students in ROTC received military training. They wore uniforms on campus. When they graduated, they could become U.S. Army officers.

Colin Powell signed up for ROTC in the fall of 1954. He joined the Pershing Rifles drill team. He did not plan to make the army his career. He thought he might serve just two years after college. As it turned out, Powell had found his life's work.

Powell liked ROTC. He enjoyed the physical activity. He liked the discipline and the teamwork. He worked hard in ROTC. He found that he was very good at it. Powell gained the rank of cadet colonel. This was the highest rank a cadet could earn.

In 1958, Powell graduated from college. He was at the top of his ROTC class. He became a second lieutenant in the army. He earned $60 a week.

Powell was sent to Fort Benning, Georgia, for basic training. Here he got a taste of the segregation laws of the South. Black soldiers and white soldiers had the same rights on the base. But black soldiers had to be careful when they went to town.

One day, Powell went to a restaurant in town. He ordered a hamburger. The waitress said that she couldn't serve him because he was black. She sent him to the back door of the restaurant. She could hand the hamburger out the door to him. Powell told her he wasn't that hungry.

After the Civil Rights Act was passed in 1964, no one could refuse service to a person based on his or her race. So, one day Powell went back to that same restaurant to get his hamburger.

In the meantime, Powell was sent to West Germany in 1959. First he was a platoon leader. Then he commanded a rifle company. By the time he returned to the United States in 1960, he was a first lieutenant.

Next, Powell was sent to Fort Devens in Massachusetts. There he met a girl named Alma Johnson. In 1962, the couple got married. They later had three children.

A few months after his marriage, Colin Powell was sent to fight in the Vietnam War. In this war, communist North Vietnam was trying to take over South Vietnam. The United States wanted to help the South Vietnamese. Powell was wounded in action twice. He received two Purple Hearts.

Powell served in Vietnam from 1962 to 1963. He then returned to the United States. He enrolled in the army's Command and General Staff College. This was at Fort Leavenworth, Kansas. He graduated second in a class of 1,244. Then the army sent him back to Vietnam in 1968.

By this time, there were 500,000 American troops in Vietnam. Things were going very badly in the war. The United States sent more and more high-tech weapons and equipment. More and more Americans were being killed or wounded. The war still did not end. Many Americans were angry about the war. They wanted the troops to come home. They felt as if the war was not for the Americans to fight.

In 1969, Powell's second tour in Vietnam ended. He returned to the States. The army sent him to graduate school. Colin Powell went to work on an MBA (Master of Business Administration) at George Washington University. This was in Washington, D.C. Powell said, "Good business managers are needed in the Department of Defense!"

In 1972, Powell's career got a big boost. He was one of seven people (out of 1,500 applicants) to be chosen as a White House Fellow. White House Fellows work for one year as assistants in a high level of the government. Fellows often later go on to work in high-level jobs in the government.

Powell worked as a special assistant to the deputy director of the Office of Management and Budget (OMB). The OMB helps the U.S. President put together the country's budget each year. It also controls how the budget is carried out.

Powell did an outstanding job at the OMB. Two important men noticed his competence. Frank Carlucci and Caspar Weinburger became his strongest supporters. They would later recommend him for higher-level jobs.

Over time, Powell rose higher in rank. In 1979, he became a brigadier general. He did many important jobs for the army. In 1989, he was promoted to four-star general. That same year he became chairman of the Joint Chiefs of Staff (JCS).

The chairman of the JCS is the main military advisor to the President. He assists the President and the Secretary of Defense. Together they decide on military actions and strategies. He is also the leader of all active-duty and reserve members of the U.S. armed forces (3–4 million troops).

Powell has worked to solve the international conflicts involving the United States since the Vietnam War. Some of these are Panama, Iraq's invasion of Kuwait, Kosovo, the Middle East, and the war on terrorism.

Powell always preferred to use diplomacy rather than force. As a soldier, he knew that sometimes military force must be used. If military action was necessary, he preferred to strike with great force to resolve the situation quickly.

On August 2, 1990, the army of Iraq invaded Kuwait. The President of Iraq was Saddam Hussein. He wanted to control Kuwait's oil fields. Powell advised President George H. W. Bush to act quickly. Powell made plans for Operation Desert Storm. He organized a buildup of troops, planes, tanks, and ships in the Middle East. Eighteen countries joined in the effort. Powell said, "My job is to make sure that if it is necessary to go to war, we go to war to win." At the same time, he tried to resolve the problem peacefully.

The United Nations Security Council gave Hussein a deadline of January 15, 1991, to remove his troops from Kuwait. Hussein did not withdraw his troops. An air attack on Iraq began 24 hours later. By February 23, Iraq had suffered major losses. Then the U.S.-led ground troops went in and continued the fight. Hussein agreed to withdraw from Kuwait.

The victory in Desert Storm was quick and decisive. Few American lives were lost. Colin Powell and the U.S. military were national heroes. Many people began to talk about Colin Powell as the next U.S. President. Powell said he had no interest in running for office.

In 1993, Powell retired as chairman of the JCS. He took two years to write his autobiography, *My American Journey.* He toured the country signing his book. Powell became more popular than ever. Again, he was mentioned as a presidential candidate.

Whenever he could, Powell made room in his schedule to visit schools. He told black students, "Don't let being black be an excuse.... If you work hard... success will come your way. I remember the feeling that you can't make it. But you can." He used himself as an example. He called himself "a black kid of no early promise and limited means."

Powell became the chairman of America's Promise—The Alliance for Youth. The group works to get adults involved in the lives of America's young people. It is based on five supports that Powell feels young people need to succeed in life. They need caring adults and safe places. They need a healthy start and a good education. They need chances to help others. Powell's wife, Alma, is also involved in America's Promise. She wrote a children's book called *America's Promise* that was published in 2003.

On December 16, 2000, President George W. Bush chose Colin Powell as his Secretary of State. Powell was sworn into office in on January 20, 2001. In this job, Powell was the President's chief foreign-affairs advisor. The first test Powell faced was the September 11, 2001, attacks on the World Trade Center and the Pentagon.

Powell organized leaders from around the world. They joined together to fight terrorism. This international battle still continues.

In February 2003, President George W. Bush asked Colin Powell to address the United Nations. He hoped to win the support of other countries to deal with difficulties rising in Iraq. It was a historic presentation.

In 2004, Powell retired. He said, "In one generation we have moved from denying a black man service at a lunch counter to elevating one to the highest military office in the nation and to being a serious contender for the presidency. This is a magnificent country, and I am proud to be one of its sons."

Remembering the Facts

1. Name two jobs that Colin Powell was the first black to hold.

2. Why did Colin Powell like ROTC?

3. What is a White House Fellow?

4. What is the job of the chairman of the Joint Chiefs of Staff?

5. What was Operation Desert Storm?

6. What is America's Promise—The Alliance for Youth?

7. What is the job of the U.S. Secretary of State?

8. What problem did Powell encounter during basic training when he tried to buy a hamburger off base?

Understanding the Story

9. Why do you think the army sent Colin Powell to graduate school?

10. Why do you think Powell preferred to use diplomacy rather than force?

Getting the Main Idea

In what ways do you think Colin Powell is a good role model for young Americans?

Applying What You've Learned

Do you think a military leader would make a good U.S. president? Write a paragraph explaining your opinion.

Benjamin Carson

Physician

Benjamin Carson is a famous neurosurgeon. A neurosurgeon is a doctor who does surgery on parts of the nervous system. Some neurosurgeons specialize in brain surgery. This is what Ben Carson does. He takes on cases that other doctors say are hopeless. He has saved the lives of many very ill children.

Carson operates on more than 300 children a year. He is world famous for his work separating conjoined twins. (The bodies of these twins are fused together.) He also came up with a surgery to help people who have seizures (sudden attacks) that can't be controlled.

Carson became director of pediatric (children's) neurosurgery at Johns Hopkins Hospital in 1984. At 33 years old, he was the youngest doctor ever to hold this job.

Benjamin Carson was born September 18, 1951, in Detroit, Michigan. He had one older brother, Curtis. Ben's father worked in a car factory. He left the family when Ben was eight years old.

Ben's mother, Sonya Carson, moved her boys to Boston. They lived with family for two years. In 1960, they went back to Detroit. There they lived in an apartment in a run-down neighborhood.

Sonya Carson had 23 brothers and sisters. She had married when she was 13. Ben's father had been 28. Sonya had only a third-grade education. She supported her family by babysitting and cleaning houses. She worked hard to give her boys a better life.

As a boy, Ben was not a good student. In fifth grade, he was the worst student in the class. He failed nearly every test. The other kids made fun of him. Ben decided he must be "dumb." He also decided that being black meant "the world was stacked against [him]."

Things were about to change. One day, the school gave students free eye exams. Ben could only read the top letter on the eye chart. The next day, he got glasses. When he wore them to class, he was amazed. Now he could see the writing on the board. His grades began to inch up.

Sonya Carson came up with a plan to help him improve more. First, she told her boys they could only watch three television shows a week. Next, they had to read at least two books each week. She had them write reports on the books they read.

Ben and Curtis were not happy with their mother's plan. Ben had never read a whole book in his life. He didn't think he could do it. But the boys did what their mother said.

Ben found he enjoyed reading about animals, nature, and science. By the end of the year, he became the class science expert. His vocabulary, spelling, and comprehension had improved greatly.

Ben entered Wilson Junior High at the top of his class. His classmates no longer teased him. Instead, they asked him for help with their work. Ben finally realized that he was very smart.

Ben had another problem. He had a bad temper. When he got mad, he would snap and lash out. One day, he and a friend were listening to the radio. The friend flipped to a station Ben didn't like. Ben grabbed the camping knife he carried in his back pocket. He thrust the knife at his friend's stomach. The blade hit his friend's belt buckle and broke off. Ben realized he had nearly killed his friend.

He ran home. He locked himself in the bathroom and sat there for hours. Ben was raised a Christian. After a while, he began to read the Bible. He read, "He who is slow to anger is better than the mighty. And he who rules his spirit (is better) than he who takes a city." (Proverbs 16:32) From that day on, Ben controlled his temper.

In high school, Ben joined the Reserve Officers' Training Corps (ROTC). During his senior year, he was captain of all the ROTC units in Detroit. He was offered an appointment to West Point military academy. West Point trains officers for the U.S. Army. Ben turned it down. He wanted to become a doctor instead.

In 1969, Ben won a scholarship to Yale University. There were many good students at Yale. Ben had trouble keeping up in his classes. He had never learned good study skills in high school.

One night he was up late studying for a chemistry exam. If he failed the test, he would have to leave Yale. Ben worked and worked, but it seemed hopeless. He felt he would never be able to learn the material in time. He even prayed for help.

Ben closed the chemistry book. He fell asleep. As he slept, he dreamed about the chemistry professor reviewing problems on the board. The next morning, he took the test. The questions on the test were the same ones Ben had dreamed about. He passed the test.

Ben Carson stayed at Yale. He learned how to study. He graduated in 1973 with a degree in psychology. He went to the medical school at the University of Michigan.

The summer before starting medical school, Carson worked at a steel company. His job was to operate a crane. He had to pick up stacks of steel that weighed tons. Then he put the stacks on waiting trucks.

While doing this job, Carson learned that he had excellent hand-eye coordination. This is a skill a good surgeon needs. People later told Carson he had "gifted hands."

Carson worked hard his first two years in medical school. He studied from 6:00 A.M. to 11:00 P.M. He worked until he knew every fact in his books.

In his third year, he began doing rotations. In rotations, the students observed different areas of medicine. Each rotation lasted a month. Rotations helped the students decide which area of medicine they liked best.

One day, Carson was watching an operation during his neurosurgery rotation. The surgeon described how hard it was to find the foramen ovale (a little hole at the base of the skull). Carson thought about this for a while. Then he came up with a new way to make it easy for surgeons to find the hole. He decided then to become a neurosurgeon.

In 1975, Ben Carson married Candy Rustin. The two had met earlier as students at Yale. They later had three sons.

In 1977, Carson graduated from medical school. From 1978 to 1983, he was an assistant resident and then a resident at Johns Hopkins. This was in Baltimore, Maryland. He was one of two medical students who were accepted out of 125 applicants.

Ben and Candy went to Australia in 1983. He gained a lot of valuable experience doing brain surgery. Then in 1984, he returned to Johns Hopkins. He became the director of pediatric neurosurgery.

In 1987, Carson made medical history. Patrick and Benjamin Binder were twins from Germany. They were joined at the back of their heads at birth. In the past, operations to separate such twins had always failed. One or both of the twins had always died. Still, Carson agreed to do the surgery to separate the boys.

A team of 70 doctors, nurses, and technicians was assembled. Five months of planning came next. Several practice runs were held. In the end, the operation took 22 hours. It was a success! Both twins were saved. Dr. Benjamin Carson gained worldwide fame.

Carson has separated many other sets of twins. In 1997, Carson went to South Africa to separate two boys joined at the top of their heads. The 28-hour operation also had a happy ending.

Carson has also performed many surgeries to help people who have seizures that cannot be controlled. To do this, he removes half of the person's brain. Nearly all patients stop having seizures after this procedure. The remaining half of the brain then begins to do the work of the missing half.

Carson also works on many cases of traumatic brain injury. He removes brain and spinal-cord tumors. Carson even developed a way to do brain surgery on a baby before it is born.

In 1990, Carson wrote his autobiography. It is called *Gifted Hands: The Ben Carson Story*. His book is read in schools across the country.

Carson followed this with *THINK BIG* in 1992. In this book, he shares his formula for success in life. He wrote a third book, *The Big Picture*, published in 1999.

Today Ben Carson is in demand as a speaker. He especially likes to talk to young people who are at risk for failure. He gives them his rules for success. He calls his rules THINK BIG. The letters stand for:

T—Talents/time: Recognize them as gifts.

H—Hope for good things and be honest.

I—Insight from people and good books.

N—Be nice to all people.

K—Knowledge: Recognize it as the key to living.

B—Books: Read them actively.

I—In-depth learning skills: Develop them.

G—God: Never get too big for Him.

Carson has won many awards and honors. He is on the board of America's Promise. (See the story on Colin Powell). He and his wife founded the Carson Scholars Fund. The Fund awards college scholarships to students of all backgrounds. Carson hopes to help students in the same way his mother helped him.

On his Web site, Carson says, "Whatever one's handicaps or hardships in life, [people] can choose how to respond to difficulties. We do not have to be the victim of circumstances, no matter how grim."

In his book *THINK BIG*, Carson says, "Young folks need to know that the way to escape their often dismal situations is within themselves. They can't expect other people to do it for them." Benjamin Carson is a fine example of someone who overcame obstacles to make it big.

Remembering the Facts

1. Why did Ben Carson think he was "dumb" in grade school?

2. What two things did Sonya Carson do to help Ben succeed in school?

3. What behavior problem did Ben Carson have to overcome?

4. What ability did Carson discover he had while operating a crane?

5. What historic operation did Carson perform in 1987?

6. What operation does Carson do to stop uncontrollable seizures?

7. What is the title of Carson's autobiography?

8. What does Carson call his rules for success?

Understanding the Story

9. Why do you think Carson says his mother played an important role in his life?

10. Explain why you think Carson likes to speak to young people who are at risk for failure.

Getting the Main Idea

In what ways do you think Ben Carson is a good role model for today's youth?

Applying What You've Learned

Make a chart in which you explain Carson's motto: THINK BIG.

Morgan Freeman

Actor

Morgan Freeman is a famous American actor. He has played many different roles. A prisoner. A washed-up boxer. A Union Army sergeant. President of the United States. A driver for an elderly woman. Even God. The roles are very different. It's hard to imagine one man playing them all. Morgan Freeman has an amazing range of acting ability. He has been called one of the greatest American actors of all time.

Freeman was over 50 years old when he became a star. He struggled for years doing small roles. Often he didn't have enough money to eat or to pay rent. At one time, he nearly gave up acting to become a taxi driver.

Morgan Freeman was born in Memphis, Tennessee, on June 1, 1937. He was the fourth of five children. When Morgan was two years old, his parents and two older brothers moved to Chicago. Morgan and his younger sister were sent to Charleston, Mississippi. There, they lived with their grandmother, Evelyn Freeman.

When Morgan was six, his grandmother died. Morgan and his sister went to live with their parents in Chicago. After six months, his parents split up. Morgan, his sister, and his mother moved back to Mississippi. They lived with his mother's mother, Lenora Revere. Morgan's father and older brothers stayed in Chicago. Morgan rarely saw his father after that.

Three years later, Morgan's mother took her children back to Chicago. They lived in one room with a gas stove. Morgan couldn't believe how cold it was. In the winter, the family used the window ledge for a freezer.

It was a hard time in Morgan's life. The family lived in a tough neighborhood. Morgan did his best to stay out of street gangs. He didn't like to fight because he didn't like to hurt people.

Morgan was lucky to have good teachers. They told him he had what it took to succeed. One teacher gave Morgan the title role in the school play, *Little Boy Blue*.

When Morgan was 11, the family moved to Gary, Indiana. Soon his mother became ill. The family moved back to Greenwood, Mississippi. They lived with Morgan's grandmother Revere.

While he was growing up, Morgan fell in love with movies. In those days, a movie ticket cost 12 cents. He earned the money he needed to buy tickets. He sold empty bottles back to the grocery store. A milk bottle was worth 5 cents. Soda bottles were worth 2 cents. Morgan found enough empty bottles to get a movie ticket nearly every day that he wasn't in school. The first movie he remembers seeing was *King Kong*. He also enjoyed watching World War II movies.

In junior high, Morgan appeared in a school play. The play won the state drama competition. Morgan was named best actor.

In high school, Morgan decided he wanted to be a fighter pilot. The war movies he'd seen made it look exciting. Morgan graduated from Greenwood High School in 1955. He turned down a scholarship to Jackson State College. He joined the U.S. Air Force.

Freeman did not become a pilot. He was a radar technician instead. This ground job bored him. After his time was up, Freeman left the Air Force. He headed to Hollywood to become an actor.

Freeman went to Paramount Studios to "sign up" for an acting job. He soon found out he couldn't get a part in a movie by filling out an application. He ended up taking a job as a clerk. He took acting classes at night.

A year later, he moved to New York City. He planned to break in to the big-time acting world. He had no luck and little to eat. After a few months, he moved to San Francisco. There he found a job with a musical theater company called the Opera Ring. He worked with this group for several years.

Freeman headed back to New York City. Now that he was more experienced, he was able to land some theater jobs. In 1968, he appeared on Broadway in an all-black version of *Hello, Dolly!* More plays followed. He also met and, in 1967, married his first wife, Jeanette Adair Bradshaw. In 1971, they had a daughter. He also adopted Jeanette's daughter.

In 1971, Freeman got the role of Easy Reader on the PBS show *The Electric Company*. This was an educational show. It was geared toward children who were learning to read. He worked on this show for five years.

Freeman was happy to have a regular paycheck. He needed to support his young family. He also liked working with the show's cast. He especially enjoyed Bill Cosby. But after a while, he felt trapped in the job. It became boring. He had personal struggles. His marriage ended.

Freeman pulled himself together. He continued acting in many Off-Broadway productions. In 1979, he won his first Obie Award for *Coriolanus*. (An Obie is an award for excellence in Off-Broadway theater.)

He won a second Obie in 1980 for *Mother Courage and Her Children*. A third came in 1984 for *The Gospel at Colonus*. That same year, he married his second wife, Myrna Colley-Lee. She was a costume and set designer. Their marriage lasted until 2008.

In 1980, Freeman had his first important movie role. He played the part of a prison inmate in *Brubaker*. This film was about corruption in

Arkansas prisons in the 1960s. It was not a well-written script. But Freeman gave an outstanding performance. Pauline Kael was a famous movie critic for the *New Yorker* magazine. She gave Freeman a great review.

In 1987, Freeman played the part of a hoodlum named Fast Black in the movie *Street Smart*. Again, critic Pauline Kael reviewed his movie. In her review, she asked, "Is Morgan Freeman America's greatest actor?"

For his role as Fast Black, Freeman was nominated for an Academy Award for Best Supporting Actor. (The Academy Awards are also called the Oscars.) Morgan Freeman had officially arrived as an actor. He was 50 years old. The same year, he won his fourth Obie for the role of Hoke Colburn in the play *Driving Miss Daisy*.

In 1989, Freeman played a tough high-school principal in the movie *Lean on Me*. Two more Freeman movies opened in 1989. The film version of *Driving Miss Daisy* won him an Oscar nomination for Best Actor. He also won praise for his role as a soldier in *Glory*.

Driving Miss Daisy takes place in 1948 in Atlanta, Georgia. It is the story of the unlikely friendship between Miss Daisy, an elderly Jewish woman, and her black driver, Hoke. At first, Miss Daisy doesn't like Hoke. Miss Daisy overcomes her prejudices in the end.

Glory is the true story of black soldiers who fought for their own freedom in the Civil War. Freeman was proud to be a part of bringing this forgotten story to light. He has said it is one of the most important movies he has ever done.

He said, "I have a special (desire) for seeing to it that (black) history is told. The black legacy is as noble, is as heroic, is as filled with adventure and conquest and discovery as anybody else's. It's just that nobody knows it. I read history as a hobby because I'm interested in my own. It's important to know so you have a sense of yourself."

In 1990, Freeman moved back to Mississippi. He had lived in New York for 25 years. He said he was ready to live "where the sun shines all the time." Freeman lives on a 125-acre ranch near Charleston, Mississippi. It is the same land his grandparents worked on years before.

Just up the road from Freeman's ranch is the small town of Clarksdale, Mississippi. It's known as the birthplace of the blues. Famous bluesmen Muddy Waters, Sam Cooke, Ike Turner, and Robert Johnson all lived in the area.

Clarksdale had few businesses or jobs. Freeman wanted to "give back" to his home state. So he started a gourmet restaurant called Madidi.

In 2001, Freeman started the Ground Zero Blues Club in Clarksdale. The club is located next to the Delta Blues Museum.

Freeman says he feels most at home in the Mississippi Delta. He has put his money and his heart into rebuilding the area following Hurricane Katrina. He is committed to helping his home state revive.

Freeman's hobby is sailing. He owns a 38-foot boat called *Sojourner*. He named the sailboat after Sojourner Truth. She was a 19th-century black and women's rights activist. He says that sailing gives him a dose of reality. It is a break from the make-believe world of acting.

In 2002, at age 65, Freeman earned his pilot's license. He and a friend bought a twin-engine Cessna together. Freeman had finally realized his dream of flying.

That same year, he starred in the movie *The Sum of All Fears*. He played a CIA director dealing with terrorists. In 2003, Freeman played God in *Bruce Almighty*. He played the same role in 2007 in *Evan Almighty*.

In 2004, Freeman starred in *Million Dollar Baby*. He played a former boxer who helps a trainer mold a young woman into a successful fighter. For this role, he won an Academy Award for Best Supporting Actor.

Freeman keeps working. In his 70s, he has several movies in the works. He also wants to keep working in theater.

Freeman set up the Rock River Foundation. Through it he has given millions of dollars to causes he supports. Most of these are centered on the Mississippi Delta. He supports 4-H clubs. He also supports Teach for America and other educational causes. He has four children and, as of this writing, ten grandchildren.

For all his fame, Freeman does not see himself as a star. He calls himself a character actor. One thing is for sure: When Morgan Freeman plays a character, no one will forget it.

Remembering the Facts

1. Name three movies Morgan Freeman has starred in.

2. Why was Morgan Freeman's childhood unsettled?

3. How did Morgan pay for tickets to the movies?

4. Why did Morgan want to become a fighter pilot?

5. What role did Freeman play for five years on *The Electric Company?*

6. Why did Freeman feel that *Glory* was an important movie?

7. Name a business Freeman started in Clarksdale, Mississippi.

8. Name a cause Freeman has supported through his foundation.

Understanding the Story

9. Why do you think Freeman thinks of himself as a character actor instead of a star?

10. Why do you think Freeman's unsettled childhood might have helped him become a better actor?

Getting the Main Idea

In what ways do you think Morgan Freeman is a good role model for young Americans?

Applying What You've Learned

Make a list of qualities you think an actor or actress needs to succeed.

Geoffrey Canada
Social Activist

Geoffrey Canada grew up in the slums of New York. He says, "I remember feeling small and scared. I remember growing up in the South Bronx." Canada knows violence is a part of the daily lives of many children. He knows how harsh the inner-city culture can be. He has lived through it.

When he grew up, Canada returned to the rough neighborhoods of his childhood. Saving the children living there became his life's work. Canada is now CEO of the Harlem Children's Zone. The Zone serves more than 8,000 children living in poverty. It is centered on nearly 100 New York City blocks in the Harlem section of the city.

The Zone offers many services. It provides education. It helps build the community. It provides social services. Children from birth through college age are included. Canada hopes to support Harlem's children in large numbers.

Geoffrey Canada was born on January 13, 1952, in New York City. He was the third of four brothers. His father was an alcoholic. He left his family when Geoffrey was four years old. Geoffrey rarely saw him after that.

Geoffrey's mother, Mary, supported her family. She worked at low-wage jobs. Sometimes she went on welfare. Often the family got food from charities. The boys never had enough clothes. Geoffrey remembers being cold because his clothing was so thin.

Mary Canada taught her boys good values. She taught them that they were responsible for their own actions. She taught them to value education and reading. She tutored her boys after school. She didn't let them watch much television. She also took them to museums and civil rights marches.

Geoffrey was an excellent student. He loved to read. Growing up in his neighborhood, he needed street smarts more than book smarts. He learned the code of the streets from the older boys on his block. He learned how to protect himself by fighting. When he was nine years old, he decided he would help poor children like himself when he grew up.

One day, he found a knife on the street. He put it in his pocket. He never showed it to anyone. Later he was playing around with the knife. He cut his right index finger to the bone. He hid the injury from his mother. He knew she would take away the knife. The finger did not heal properly. To this day, the end of his finger is bent inward.

Geoffrey never had the finger repaired. He said in his book, *Fist Stick Knife Gun: A Personal History of Violence in America*, "The finger keeps the (importance) of the work ... I do with children at the front of my mind. The slight deformity is such a small price to have paid for growing up in the South Bronx. So many others have paid with their lives."

When Geoffrey was a teenager, he had a lot of anger issues. So, his mother sent him to live with his grandparents. They lived in Freeport, Long Island, just east of New York City. Both of them were Baptist ministers. His grandmother helped Geoffrey lose the anger he felt. She taught him to value life over material things. She gave him back his faith. It had nearly been destroyed on the streets.

Geoffrey attended Wyandanch Memorial High School. Nearly all the students at the school were black. His senior year he won a scholarship to Bowdoin College in Brunswick, Maine. Bowdoin is a small liberal arts college with a good academic reputation. Geoffrey arrived at Bowdoin for his freshman year. He was shocked to realize that the school was 95 percent white and 100 percent male. (The school is now more racially diverse and has both male and female students.)

Geoffrey began to like Bowdoin. He received a lot of attention from his professors. His classmates were helpful and caring. Geoffrey majored in psychology and sociology. He also took education courses. He graduated from Bowdoin in 1974. In 1975, he earned a master's degree in education from the Harvard Graduate School of Education.

In 1975, Geoffrey Canada began teaching at the Robert White School in Boston. This was a private school for emotionally disturbed teens. Most of them were white. In *Fist Stick Knife Gun*, Canada said, "The school was the last stop before jail or a locked psychiatric hospital. It was for teenagers from the Boston slums. By and large, they were just like the kids I had grown up with in the Bronx. They were poor, angry, estranged from society … and (focused on) violence." Canada was gifted in handling the students. In 1977, he became director of the school.

Canada is a third-degree black belt. In 1983, he moved back to New York City and founded the Chang Moo Kwan Martial Arts School. He teaches his students tai kwon do. He emphasizes self-defense. He says this is the best way to prevent violence. The school offers lessons for free. Canada himself has taught there two nights a week for more than two decades.

In 1983, Canada began working at Rheedlen Centers for Children and Families in Harlem. He became director of the truancy prevention program. The Centers had after-school programs. They did truancy prevention and anti-violence training. In 1990, Canada became president and CEO of Rheedlen.

Under Canada's guidance, the programs at Rheedlen grew. The number of children served increased from 1,500 to more than 7,000. This was good. But Canada knew that the Centers were not reaching all the children who needed help. There was a long waiting list to get in. This upset Canada. He felt he was saving some kids but losing the rest. The ones he couldn't reach might repeat the cycle of poverty and violence.

Canada decided that a new approach was needed. He would no longer work on just part of the problem. He would attack the problem on three fronts.

The first front was education. He would offer help to schools. He would set up good day-care and after-school programs. These things would ensure a better education for children.

The second front was building stronger families. Parent training would be provided. Counseling would be available for parents who needed it. Parents would learn how to teach their children good values.

The third front was changing the "ghetto mindset." He pointed out that many children growing up in poor neighborhoods feel helpless. They feel that the problems are too big to fix. If people expect to fail in life, they do. Canada said, "If we can get Harlem to the place where passing is the normal thing, staying out of jail is normal, boys growing up and getting jobs is normal, that is victory."

The New York Times called Canada's three-pronged approach "one of the most ambitious social experiments of our time." Indeed, it was an idea that had never been tried before.

Canada proposed his idea to the board of the Rheedlen Centers in 1998. He told them he wanted to totally change the way the Centers worked. He ended up having to get mostly new board members before he could carry out his plan.

Stan Druckenmiller became the new chairman of the board. He had gone to Bowdoin College with Canada. Druckenmiller was a very successful businessman on Wall Street. He agreed with Canada's vision for Harlem. The name of the project was changed from Rheedlen Centers to the Harlem Children's Zone.

Druckenmiller and Canada convinced Wall Street managers to serve on the board. Today about one-third of the yearly budget of the Zone comes from the board members themselves. The rest comes from other individual gifts, foundations, and the government.

Canada decided that he would start small. He would center his plan in one 24-block area of Harlem. More than 3,400 children lived there. Nearly all of them lived in poverty. They had low math and reading scores on tests. Canada called the area the Harlem Children's Zone. (In 2004, the Zone was expanded to 60 city blocks. By 2007, the Zone covered nearly 100 blocks.)

The Harlem Children's Zone includes about 20 educational, social, and medical programs. It employs more than 1,200 workers.

Paul Tough of *The New York Times* describes the Zone: "It starts at birth and follows children to college. It meshes those services into a web. Then it drops that web over an entire neighborhood. It operates on the principle that each child will do better if all the children around him are doing better.... The objective is to create a safety net woven so tightly that children in the neighborhood just can't slip through."

Zone employees don't sit around waiting for people to sign up for its programs. They search the neighborhood, signing people up. Sometimes they offer prizes to get people started. For example, parents who complete the Baby College (parent training classes) receive small gifts. They are entered into a drawing for a month's free rent.

In 2004, Canada opened the HCZ Promise Academy. The Academy is a charter school. Classes are small. Teachers use different teaching methods to reach the students. The school runs 1 ½ hours longer per day than other New York schools. It has 30 more days in the school year.

Canada has said, "We are calling our school Promise Academy. This is because we are making a promise to all of our parents. If your child is in our school, we will guarantee that child succeeds. There will be no excuses. If your child goes to our school, that child is going to succeed."

Canada has written about growing up in the South Bronx. In 1995, his book *Fist Stick Knife Gun: A Personal History of Violence in America*, was published.

Canada's book *Reaching Up for Manhood: Transforming the Lives of Boys in America*, was published in 1998. In this book, he talks about the wrong ideas boys have about how to be a man. He talks about the need for men to be good fathers. He talks about the importance of good male role models for boys.

Canada has received many awards and honors. In 1995, he received the Heinz Award. This includes a cash prize of $250,000. In 2005, he was named "One of America's Best Leaders" by *U.S. News & World Report*. In 2006, he was named co-chair of a task force to reduce poverty in New York City.

The Harlem Children's Zone has become a model for the nation. Canada has been featured on many television programs. His work has been written about in newspapers and magazines. He is in demand as a speaker around the nation. Canada is also married and has four children.

In *Fist Stick Knife Gun*, Canada said, "I want to be a children's hero. Children need heroes because heroes give hope. Without hope, they have no future." Geoffrey Canada is a man of hope and love. He has dedicated his life to helping poor children. His passion is to make their lives safer and more successful.

Remembering the Facts

1. What three types of programs does the Harlem Children's Zone include?

2. What values did Mary Canada teach her children?

3. Why has Canada never had the injury to his finger repaired?

4. How did Canada's grandmother help him recover from his life on the streets?

5. What lesson does Canada teach children through the martial arts?

6. Why was Canada not satisfied with his success with the Rheedlen Centers?

7. What are the three approaches Canada takes in attacking problems in the Zone?

8. What promise does Canada make to the parents of students at the Promise Academy?

Understanding the Story

9. Why do you think Canada says that a combination of three approaches is needed to fix the problems faced by children in the Zone?

10. In *Fist Stick Knife Gun,* Canada wrote, "Children need heroes because heroes give hope. Without hope, they have no future." What do you think he meant?

Getting the Main Idea

In what ways do you think that Geoffrey Canada is a good role model for young Americans?

Applying What You've Learned

Think of an area that could benefit from a program such as the Harlem Children's Zone. It could be an area in your town or somewhere else. Write a paragraph telling why you think the Zone could help children in this area.

Ruth Simmons

University President

Ruth Simmons is president of Brown University in Providence, Rhode Island. She is the first African-American president of an Ivy League university. It's safe to say that she is also the first Ivy League university president who was born in a sharecropper's cabin.

Simmons is respected by faculty and students. She is known as a caring and enthusiastic educator. She says that "teaching is the best thing you can do for others." She credits her past teachers for her success.

Ruth was born on July 3, 1945, in Grapeland, Texas. She was the youngest of 12 children. Her parents were sharecroppers. They worked on another person's land for a share of the crop earnings.

All the older children in the family helped pick cotton. Ruth was too young. Her job was to carry the sacks for the others. The family was very poor. They owned no books. At Christmas, each child got an orange, an apple, and ten nuts.

When Ruth was seven, the family moved to Houston, Texas. Ruth's father worked in a factory. He was also pastor of the Mount Hermon Missionary Baptist Church. Ruth's mother cleaned homes and did ironing.

The family lived in the Fifth Ward. It was a poor neighborhood. It was a hard place to live. White teenagers often threatened the black children as they walked home from school.

Ruth's parents were not well educated. Both had only finished eighth grade. But they taught their children some important lessons. Ruth's mother took her along when she cleaned homes. She took great pride in her work. When she scrubbed floors, she made sure she did the best possible job. When she ironed, she would work on each piece until it was perfect.

Ruth Simmons later said, "When I watched my mother iron those mounds of clothes and move the iron around those buttons, absolutely insisting that she do the very best job she could, that is how I learned to be a college president."

Ruth recalls her parents' values: "Do good work. Don't ever get too big for your britches. Always be an authentic person. Don't worry too much about being famous and rich, because that doesn't amount to too much."

Ruth's parents taught her self-respect. They taught by example to have courage in the face of prejudice. Ruth learned to carry herself with dignity no matter how difficult things became.

Public schools in the South were segregated when Ruth started school. The school she attended was all black. There were many caring teachers. School became a place of safety for Ruth. She learned to love books and reading. Ruth said, "My parents were suspicious about all my reading. But for me it opened a window into a different reality, where it was possible for someone like me to be accepted."

When Ruth was 15, her mother died. Ruth's teachers at Phyllis Wheatley High School helped her through this difficult time.

Ruth's drama teacher, Vernell Lillie, saw how talented Ruth was. She helped Ruth get a scholarship to study drama at Dillard University. This was a black college in New Orleans.

When it was time for Ruth to start college, one of her teachers gave her clothes from her own closet. Ruth's brothers and sisters helped out, too. They gave her small amounts of money when they could. They were so proud of her. She was the first in their family to go to college.

Ruth changed her major to French. She was chosen for an exchange program with Wellesley. This was a women's college in Massachusetts. Ruth later said that this experience totally changed her life.

At the time, all the students at Wellesley were white women. Most of them came from wealthy families. Ruth had been taught from childhood that blacks were less capable in the classroom. Ruth soon realized that was wrong.

She said, "I came to realize that my mind was just the same as the students in the classroom with me. I could do everything that these very wealthy, very well-prepared white women could do. I had sort of suspected that there wasn't very much to all this hype that blacks were inferior to whites. But now I knew the truth, and an electric bolt went through me."

In 1967, Ruth graduated from Dillard. She won a Fulbright scholarship to study at the Université de Lyon in France. By this time, she was quite fluent in French.

In 1968, Ruth married Norbert Simmons. They later had two children.

Norbert began law school at Boston University. Ruth began graduate school at nearby Harvard. She earned a master's degree and a Ph.D. in Romance languages from Harvard.

For the next ten years, Ruth Simmons's priority was her family. She went with her husband wherever he needed to go for his job. She spent her time raising her young children. She also worked part-time teaching French at the University of New Orleans.

The Simmons family moved to southern California. Ruth worked at California State University at Northridge. She also worked at the University of Southern California. In 1983, Ruth and her husband divorced. She now had two teenagers to raise.

That same year, she was hired at Princeton University. This is an Ivy League school in New Jersey. She re-organized the Black Studies Department. She hired the Nobel Prize-winning writer Toni Morrison. She also hired other famous African Americans. She served in other important positions at Princeton.

Racial incidents happened on campus in 1993. Simmons was asked to investigate. She talked to many students and faculty members. She wrote the Simmons Report to share her findings. The report offered ideas for solving and preventing future racial problems. Her ideas were adopted by many other colleges around the United States. Simmons gained nationwide fame.

In 1995, Simmons became president of Smith College. Smith is a top-quality all-women's college in Massachusetts. It's the largest women's college in the United States. At Smith, Simmons set up the first engineering program at a women's college. She doubled Smith's endowment fund. She also doubled the number of black students on campus.

Simmons was very popular with both students and faculty at Smith. When she appeared at programs on campus, the students would chant her name.

Toni Morrison said, "Ruth Simmons has an unusual combination of real politics and integrity. She has a keen sense of morals which does not interfere with her generosity and her wide spiritedness. She's extremely creative in terms of solving other people's problems. And she's a lot of fun."

In 2001, Simmons became president of Brown University. Simmons became the first African American to head an Ivy League school. In fact, very few women of any race had been university presidents.

Every year, Simmons goes back to Texas to visit her family. When she is there, she goes to schools in the inner cities. She looks for promising inner-city students who might be a good fit at Brown.

Simmons introduced needs-blind admissions at Brown. This means that students are admitted to the school regardless of their ability to pay. Scholarships then make up the difference. Simmons also hired more faculty. She worked to get more money for the school.

Simmons holds honorary degrees from many colleges. She has won a number of awards. In 2001, *Time* magazine named her America's best college president.

Ruth Simmons believes that education can change lives. She has seen this first-hand in her own life. She once said, "I'd like for every student to experience a moment of learning that is so delicious that they want to hold on to it forever."

Simmons also said, "I want to make a difference by working with students. I want to make a difference because when I was a child without means, people did that for me.... It is the care that we give to people that makes them transform their lives and do things that are quite extraordinary." Ruth Simmons has certainly achieved this goal.

Remembering the Facts

1. What kind of work did Ruth's parents do in Grapeland?

2. How did Ruth's parents teach by example?

3. Why did school become a place of safety for Ruth?

4. Name three ways people helped Ruth attend Dillard University.

5. Why did Ruth say that her experience at Wellesley changed her life?

6. What was the Simmons Report?

7. What program did Simmons start at Smith College?

8. What university position did Simmons earn in 2001?

Understanding the Story

9. Why do you think Ruth Simmons believes in the power of education to change lives?

10. Why do you think Simmons started a needs-blind admissions policy at Brown?

Getting the Main Idea

In what ways do you think Ruth Simmons is a good role model for young Americans?

Applying What You've Learned

List five values you learned as a young child. Why do you think these values would still be important for you as an adult?

Vocabulary

Langston Hughes

poet laureate	injustice	Great Depression	deferred
Harlem Renaissance	spirituals	military	fester
	bar exam	epic poem	inducted

Jesse Owens

sharecropper	equality	Nazi party	honorary
pneumonia	interscholastic	goodwill	inducted
Olympics	inequality	ambassador	

Benjamin O. Davis Jr.

military	cockpit	tenacity	destroyer
squadron	nominate	infantry	sky marshal
regiment	cadet	escort	
barnstormer			

Fannie Lou Hamer

registration	baptize	Ku Klux Klan	convention
plantation	spirituals	application	honorary doctorate
sharecropper	register	civil rights	co-op
polio	literacy	delegate	ambassador
paralysis	poll tax		

Coretta Scott King

justice	missionary	nonviolent	legacy
Great Depression	scholarship	pastor	honorary doctorate
racism	boycott	riot	

Alex Haley

heritage	publication	epic	memorial
Coast Guard	journalist	miniseries	symbolize
messboy	interview	Pulitzer Prize	descendant
rejection	research	ethnic	triumph
mess hall			

Muhammad Ali

heavyweight	Nation of Islam	Sunni	opponent
injustice	Muslim	draft	humanitarian
prejudice	racism	evasion	

Faith Ringgold

quilting	fashion design	realism	commemorate
asthma	honorary	exhibition	illustrator
hone	doctorate	mural	

Alice Walker

Pulitzer Prize	creativity	register
sharecropper	delegate	consultant
independence	registration	writer-in-residence
self-sufficiency		

Gladys Knight

amateur	venue	symbolic	AIDS
Chitlin' Circuit	segregation	integration	inducted
gig	discriminate	Grammy	diabetes

Vocabulary

Bernice Johnson Reagon

justice	a cappella	afros	Grammy
historian	spirituals	doctoral thesis	humanities
curator emeritus	hymns	administration	injustice
registration	contralto	culture	

Colin Powell

stickball	segregation	brigadier general	diplomacy
military	platoon	strategy	candidate
cadet colonel	communist	international	alliance
lieutenant	Purple Heart	conflict	magnificent

Benjamin Carson

neurosurgeon	pediatric	resident	tumor
conjoined twins	hand-eye	traumatic	
seizure	coordination		

Morgan Freeman

technician	Oscar	gourmet
corruption	prejudice	Obie Award nominate
Academy Award	legacy	Cessna

Geoffrey Canada

slum	deformity	sociology	estranged
alcoholic	liberal arts	psychiatric	truancy
welfare	psychology	tai kwon do	charter school

Ruth Simmons

Ivy League	pastor	fluent	needs-blind
sharecropper	authentic	priority	admission
faculty	prejudice	endowment	honorary
enthusiastic	segregated	integrity	

Answer Key

Langston Hughes

Remembering the Facts

1. He was not allowed to take the bar exam after he had studied to be a lawyer.
2. He felt alone and isolated from his parents and other people. He wrote poems as a way to express his feelings.
3. It talks about the flow of events in Langston's life and the flow of events in the history of black people.
4. Langston had great success selling his poems and stories in the year after he graduated from high school.
5. It was a time in the 1920s when there was great activity in the arts and music among African Americans. The activity was centered in Harlem, a part of New York City.
6. (any two) Countee Cullen, Zora Neale Hurston, James Weldon Johnson
7. He wrote about equal rights for blacks in the military.
8. (any one) life in Harlem; what might happen if people are not allowed to pursue their dreams

Understanding the Story

9. He talks about how blacks might feel. He writes about civil rights issues. He writes about places blacks lived and about things they did.
10. The dream could dry up and go away. It could become a burden. Or it might cause the person to "blow up" or deteriorate in other ways.

Getting the Main Idea

He had the courage to pursue his dream of being a poet. He used his gift of writing to express the feelings of blacks and their need to gain civil rights. He used his writing to speak out against injustice.

Applying What You've Learned

Poems will vary.

Jesse Owens

Remembering the Facts

1. farming land owned by another person in exchange for part of the crop earnings
2. It was something you could do by yourself with no equipment needed. You were in control of what you did.
3. (any two) Push himself to the limit. Look to the future. Work for steady improvement. Run to beat his own times. Run like a race horse.
4. He set a world record and tied another world record.
5. long jump, 220-yard dash, 220-yard low hurdles
6. The Nazis believed that white Germans were superior to all other people. Hitler thought the German Olympians would prove this by defeating Owens.
7. Because of World War II, there were no Olympics in 1940 or 1944.
8. AP named him the greatest track-and-field athlete of all time.

Understanding the Story

9. It showed that athletes of any race could engage in friendly competition.
10. Owens's legacy is one of a true international sportsman. Germany's recognition of Owens as a great athlete shows the reconciliation between the United States and Germany after World War II ended the Nazi regime.

Getting the Main Idea

He worked hard to achieve his goals. He was a great athlete and a great person as well. He used his fame to work to help disadvantaged youth around the country.

Applying What You've Learned

You need to work hard to make yourself the best person you can be. By competing with yourself instead of others, you will improve yourself without putting others down. Each of us has areas of strength and weakness. To gain victory over yourself, you work to improve your strengths and diminish your weaknesses.

Benjamin O. Davis Jr.

Remembering the Facts

1. He taught military science and led ROTC units.
2. When he was 14, he took a ride with a barnstorming pilot and loved it.
3. No one spoke to him outside the line of duty. He never had a roommate. No one would eat with him.
4. They were a service unit. They did cleaning, yard work, and equipment repair.
5. President Roosevelt wanted support from black voters, so he ordered a black flying unit to be created.
6. They escorted bomber planes safely to and from their German targets.
7. none
8. Distinguished Flying Cross, Silver Star, four-star full general

Understanding the Story

9. Davis was a very patriotic man. He loved his country and wished to serve it in the military. He thought of himself as an American, not a black American.
10. His military record was outstanding and unblemished. He conducted himself well in every assignment he had. He stood up to those who discriminated against him with courage and grace. He was an excellent example of what blacks were capable of in the military. No one could refute the accomplishments of the Tuskegee Airmen led by Davis.

Getting the Main Idea

Benjamin O. Davis was steadfast and persistent in attempting to reach his goals. He was dignified under pressure. He refused to sink to the level of his attackers. He continued doing the best he could under very difficult circumstances.

Applying What You've Learned

Answers will vary.

Fannie Lou Hamer

Remembering the Facts

1. She read everything she could find.
2. The plantation owners were happy at the prospect of another field hand to work their fields.
3. the literacy test, the poll tax, threats from the Ku Klux Klan
4. She lost her job and her home. She was shot at. The Ku Klux Klan threatened her.
5. She worked to register other black voters. She spoke at mass meetings. She went to northern states to raise money for SNCC.
6. It was formed to include both black and white members, unlike the nearly all-white Democratic Party of Mississippi.
7. Hamer was seated as an official delegate from a black-and-white delegation.
8. a low-cost day-care center, better housing, a farm co-op

Understanding the Story

9. Singing is a powerful way of expressing one's feelings. Songs were sung to pass the time, as prayer, and to tell stories of the past.
10. She wanted to let her light (the goodness inside her) shine forth. She wanted to use her strong spirit to do good works and praise God.

Getting the Main Idea

She was a woman of tremendous courage and spirit. Although she had little education, she became a strong civil rights leader. She never gave up hope. She inspired millions of blacks and whites to stand up for what was right.

Applying What You've Learned

Answers will vary.

Coretta Scott King

Remembering the Facts

1. Her family's house and her father's business were burned down. Her father's mules were poisoned. She saw inequality in the education system.
2. Black children were taught in a crowded one-room school. Whites had small class sizes. Black children had to pay for books. Whites got free books. Black children had to walk to school, while white children rode on buses.
3. elementary education and music
4. They hoped to help blacks earn civil rights.
5. She gave "Freedom Concerts."
6. The Center keeps Dr. King's legacy alive by teaching about human rights and justice. It also has a large collection of civil rights documents.
7. It is given to an African-American author and an African-American illustrator whose books reflect diversity and the American dream.
8. public service

Understanding the Story

9. Some white people were fearful and racist. They did not think of blacks as equals.
10. She expanded the work of Dr. King throughout the world.

Getting the Main Idea

She was a strong woman who stood up for what she knew was right no matter what the cost. She was a person of great faith and courage.

Applying What You've Learned

Answers will vary. Suggested answers: women's and children's rights; gay rights; needs of the poor and homeless; health care; religious freedom

Alex Haley

Remembering the Facts

1. He listened to the stories told by his grandmother and her sisters.
2. He read many books. He wrote long letters to everyone he knew, as well as letters on behalf of other crew members.
3. He sold stories about the Coast Guard to *Coronet* magazine.
4. He wrote stories to promote the Coast Guard to the media.
5. He wrote a series of biographies of famous people.
6. The person being interviewed talked as long as she or he wanted to about a question. Then the interview was published as recorded.
7. No one had ever before written the story of their ancestry through slavery back to Africa.
8. He found a storyteller in Africa who knew the history of Haley's family.

Understanding the Story

9. It told the story of the Africans who were kidnapped into slavery. It made African Americans more aware of their African ancestry and proud of that culture.
10. The storyteller had memorized the history of a village, including births, deaths, and other important events. It was clear that Haley's grandmother had the same kind of memory. She could talk for days about family history.

Getting the Main Idea

He was persistently focused on achieving his dream. He worked for 12 years to achieve his goal of writing his family history, *Roots*.

Applying What You've Learned

Answers will vary.

Muhammad Ali

Remembering the Facts

1. He looked for a policeman to report the crime to and found one in a boxing gym.
2. He would throw a quick punch, then lean back out of his opponent's way.
3. He won an Olympic gold medal in boxing.
4. He became the heavyweight champion of the world.
5. He was given a new name when he became a Muslim.
6. His licenses were taken away because he refused to serve in the military.
7. He used his fame to get people to listen to what he had to say about human rights and other issues.
8. as a heavyweight champ, and as a man who was humorous, treated others right, never looked down on others, helped others, stood up for his beliefs, and tried to unite all people

Understanding the Story

9. He embodied the Olympic ideal of a great athlete and a great person.
10. Public opinion turned against the war. People admired Ali for standing up for his beliefs.

Getting the Main Idea

He achieved his goals in boxing by working hard. He then used his fame for the betterment of all humanity.

Applying What You've Learned

Poems will vary.

Faith Ringgold

Remembering the Facts

1. Doing art kept her busy when she had asthma and couldn't go to school.
2. The tar beach was the tar-covered rooftop of the family's apartment building.
3. She sewed jackets for the army and made clothing for friends and family.
4. the civil rights movement from the viewpoint of a black woman
5. A story quilt combines painting, quilting, and storytelling. The story is written in parts on sections of the quilt.
6. *Tar Beach*
7. A children's book editor saw the story quilt *Tar Beach* and knew it would make a good children's book.
8. It works to introduce children and adults to African-American artists.

Understanding the Story

9. Prior to the civil rights movement, non-whites and women were discriminated against.
10. All of her story quilts were developed to convey a story to the viewer. They also have some of the visual elements of traditional quilts.

Getting the Main Idea

Faith Ringgold kept focusing on her goal even when many people told her she would never reach it. She rejected prejudice and believed in herself.

Applying What You've Learned

Story quilts will vary.

Alice Walker

Remembering the Facts

1. They were sharecroppers.
2. By mistake, one of her brothers shot her in the eye with a BB gun.
3. She was inspired. She said his words went through her body and soul.
4. He encouraged her and included her short story in a book.
5. There were few such courses at the time. She taught her students about writers who had previously been forgotten.
6. They were a biracial couple.
7. *The Color Purple*
8. It provides summer programs and scholarships for needy children.

Understanding the Story

9. Mrs. Walker was proud of her daughter. She gave Alice meaningful gifts when she sent her off to college.
10. She took part in protests and worked to register voters. All of her experiences influenced what she wrote. She taught college-level courses that highlighted blacks and women.

Getting the Main Idea

She worked hard to reach her goals. She addressed important issues of race and women's rights.

Applying What You've Learned

Answers will vary.

Gladys Knight

Remembering the Facts

1. *The Original Amateur Hour*
2. eight years old
3. the nickname for the string of venues that were safe for black entertainers to perform in during the time of racial segregation.
4. Blacks were discriminated against. Most hotels would not rent rooms to blacks. Restaurants either refused to serve blacks or made them come to the back door to get food.
5. "I Heard It Through the Grapevine"
6. "Midnight Train to Georgia"
7. She wanted to honor those who had been friends, mentors, and sources of inspiration for her over the years.
8. to teach people to make healthy choices to live better and longer

Understanding the Story

9. Answers will vary. Responses may include that there is much competition. An artist has to find the right song to record. Then the artist has to find a company to make a recording and market the music. Being an artist also means performing often and in many locations.
10. She had a close relationship with her family. She had strong religious beliefs.

Getting the Main Idea

She has worked very hard to make her dream come true. She worked with the same group (The Pips) for close to 40 years. She has remained loyal to her friends and to her values.

Applying What You've Learned

Lyrics will vary.

Bernice Johnson Reagon

Remembering the Facts

1. As a child, Reagon sang in church, and also listened to blues music after her parents were asleep.
2. There was no piano in her church or school, so she sang unaccompanied.
3. The administration was alarmed about the civil rights demonstrations, so they expelled students who were involved.

4. Reagon saw her as a fierce warrior of the civil rights movement who used song to convey much of her powerful message.
5. "The Songs of the Civil Rights Movement, 1955–1965: A Study in Culture History"
6. justice, respect, and equality
7. how black history and culture affected black sacred music and vice versa
8. to present information about African-American history and culture to the public, so people would know the origins of various traditions

Understanding the Story

9. Their stories inspired her. She loved that they were strong women who fought for what they believed. They not only used the spoken word and brave actions, but also conveyed much of their message in song.
10. Answers will vary. A strong woman must be hard and strong on the outside like a rock. But inside, she can be sweet and kind.

Getting the Main Idea

She worked hard for the cause she believed in. She devoted her life to telling the African-American story. She used her skills for singing, teaching, and historical research to help all Americans understand black history.

Applying What You've Learned

Answers will vary.

Colin Powell

Remembering the Facts

1. U.S. Secretary of State; chairman of the Joint Chiefs of Staff
2. He liked the discipline, teamwork, and physical activity.
3. a person who works for one year as an assistant in a high level of the government
4. This person is the main military advisor to the U.S. President. He or she is also the leader of all active-duty and reserve members of the U.S. military.
5. It was an operation to force Saddam Hussein's army to leave Kuwait.
6. It is a group that seeks to involve adults in the lives of American youth in a variety of ways.
7. This person is the U.S. president's chief foreign-affairs advisor.
8. The waitress told him he would have to go to the back door to be served because he was black.

Understanding the Story

9. The military needs people in a wide variety of positions, some requiring advanced education. They send people who show promise, such as Powell did, to get advanced training.
10. Powell had seen the effects of war on both soldiers and civilians when he served in Vietnam. Because of this, he would not commit troops without trying to negotiate first.

Getting the Main Idea

Colin Powell is an excellent example of the American Dream. He grew up in modest surroundings without a lot of money. He showed little promise as a boy. But when he found his life's calling, he put everything he had into achieving as much as he could. He is clearly a man of purpose and vision. When he retired from military and government service, he put his energy into helping the youth of America.

Applying What You've Learned

Paragraphs will vary.

Benjamin Carson

Remembering the Facts

1. He got the worst grades of all the kids in his fifth-grade class.
2. She limited his TV viewing. She made him read two books a week and write reports on them.
3. He had a very bad temper, sometimes even becoming violent.
4. He had excellent hand-eye coordination.
5. He separated twins who were joined at the back of their heads.
6. He removes half of the person's brain.
7. *Gifted Hands: The Ben Carson Story*
8. THINK BIG

Understanding the Story

9. If his mother had not taken action, Ben might not have graduated from high school. He would never have developed his talents.
10. Carson realizes he was lucky to have a mother who stepped in and turned his life around. He hopes that he might be able to help another young person in the same way.

Getting the Main Idea

Answers will vary. Ben Carson came from a background in which he had few advantages. He was raised in poverty by a single mother. He grew up in a tough neighborhood. He learned how to overcome his problems and believe in himself. With persistence, hard work, and great focus, he achieved his goals.

Applying What You've Learned

Charts will vary.

Morgan Freeman

Remembering the Facts

1. (any three) *Brubaker, Street Smart, Lean on Me, Driving Miss Daisy, Glory, The Sum of All Fears, Bruce Almighty, Evan Almighty, Million Dollar Baby*
2. He moved a lot. His parents divorced. His grandmother died.
3. He collected and sold empty bottles.
4. He had seen movies about the adventures of fighter pilots in World War II.
5. Easy Reader
6. It told the forgotten story of the role played by black soldiers in the Civil War.
7. Madidi (a restaurant), the Ground Zero Blues Club
8. 4-H clubs, Teach for America, other educational causes

Understanding the Story

9. People look at a star and see only the star. People look at Freeman and see the character he is portraying.
10. He had a wide variety of experiences at an early age.

Getting the Main Idea

He kept working for many years to achieve his dream. When he reached his goal, he used his success to make things better in his hometown.

Applying What You've Learned

Answers will vary.

Geoffrey Canada

Remembering the Facts

1. education, helping build the community, social services
2. responsibility for their actions and the importance of education and reading

3. It reminds him of the dangers of growing up in the slums and the importance of the work he does with children.
4. She helped him get over his anger. She helped him regain his faith.
5. prevention of violence through self-defense
6. So many children were not being served.
7. education for the children; training for parents; changing the mindset of residents
8. He promises that all the children at this school will succeed.

Understanding the Story

9. Many programs try to fix just one facet of the problems. But social problems such as those in the ghettos are multi-faceted. Trying to fix just one cause doesn't usually work. By working to fix all causes (education, family, and community), success is much more likely.
10. Without someone to serve as a good example, children may not believe they can overcome the challenges they face. They may give up on trying to create a better future for themselves.

Getting the Main Idea

He has overcome a childhood of poverty and violence. He has used the skills he learned to help create change in communities that struggle. He provides an opportunity for people to get educational, social, and health services.

Applying What You've Learned

Answers will vary.

Ruth Simmons

Remembering the Facts

1. They were sharecroppers.
2. Her mother taught Ruth to have pride in her work and to do the very best job she could. Her parents taught her to have self-respect and courage in the face of prejudice.
3. She found many caring teachers. She also developed a love of books.
4. A teacher recommended her for a scholarship. Another teacher gave her clothes. Her brothers and sisters gave her money when they could.
5. She learned that she could think and learn as well as the wealthy white women who attended the school.
6. It described Simmons's ideas for solving and preventing racial problems on a college campus.
7. She set up the first engineering program at a women's college.
8. president of Brown University

Understanding the Story

9. Education changed her life. She was able to leave a life of poverty and hard labor and earn a Ph.D. She thinks education is the answer for other students in poverty.
10. She wanted the school to admit students based on their promise and abilities rather than looking first at their financial status.

Getting the Main Idea

She worked hard and believed in herself. She overcame many obstacles, including racial and gender discrimination. She continues to work to help young people achieve their goals.

Applying What You've Learned

Answers will vary.

Additional Activities

Langston Hughes

1. Obtain a copy of one of Langston Hughes's poems. Analyze the poem. Write about the poem and your reaction to it. Read both the poem and your analysis to the class.
2. Write one of Hughes's poems on a sheet of poster board. Illustrate the poem.
3. Research the Harlem Renaissance. Choose another writer, an artist, or a musician from the time. Write a biography of the person you selected. Share your findings with the class.

Jesse Owens

1. Create an illustrated time line showing the important events of Jesse Owens's life.
2. Find the current world-record holders in the events for which Owens earned individual Olympic gold medals: the 100-meter run, the long jump, and the 200-meter run. Graph and compare the times.
3. Look up the Jesse Owens Foundation at www.jesse-owens.org. Describe the work the Foundation is doing today.
4. Read more about Jesse Owens on his official Web site: www.jesseowens.com.

Benjamin O. Davis Jr.

1. Use the Internet to learn more about the Tuskegee Airmen. You may wish to visit the site www.tuskegeeairmen.org. Make a list of the facts you learn.
2. Watch the 1995 movie *The Tuskegee Airmen* starring Andre Braugher as Davis. Make a poster to advertise the movie.
3. Learn more about the Buffalo Soldiers. Write a report describing their duties and requirements.
4. Find out the requirements for admission to West Point (or one of the other service academies) today. Make a poster that shows these requirements.
5. Black soldiers have served in every war in U.S. history. Read more about the role of black soldiers in another war (for example, the Revolutionary War, the Civil War, or the Vietnam War). Visually represent your findings to the class.
6. Benjamin O. Davis Sr. also had an outstanding career in the army. Read more about his career. Make a time line showing his assignments.

Fannie Lou Hamer

1. Learn about voting-rights issues as they exist today.
2. Read about the Voting Rights Act of 1965. What were its key provisions? Explain your opinion of this law.
3. Listen to an African-American hymn or spiritual. Share it with the class.
4. Read more about the Student Nonviolent Coordinating Committee (SNCC). Write about your opinion of this group's work.
5. Make a word web in which you list adjectives that would describe Fannie Lou Hamer.
6. Research the history of the Ku Klux Klan and its activities. Write about your opinion of this group's work.
7. Use the Internet to research the Mississippi Freedom Democratic Party. Share your findings with the class.

Coretta Scott King

1. Read a biography of Dr. Martin Luther King Jr.
2. Use the Internet to learn more about the King Center (the Martin Luther King, Jr. Center for Nonviolent Social Change) in Atlanta at www.thekingcenter.org.
3. Find out who has won the Coretta Scott King Book Award. Make a chart listing the winners. Locate one of the books in the library. Write a report supporting why the book deserved the award.
4. Make a time line of Coretta Scott King's activities in the pursuit of social justice after 1968.
5. Mrs. King supported many causes other than black rights. Research and make a list of causes she supported. Consider why she chose to support each cause.

Alex Haley

1. Read Haley's book *Roots*. Make a time line showing the major events in the book.
2. Watch the miniseries *Roots* on DVD. Give your impressions of the series to the class.
3. Read about the Coast Guard cutter that was named for Haley. Access the Coast Guard Web site at www.uscg.mil/pacarea/cgcAlexHaley.
4. Read about the Haley Memorial in Annapolis at www.kintehaley.org/memorial.html. Write a paragraph describing your feelings about the memorial.

Muhammad Ali

1. Learn more about the Muhammad Ali Center in Louisville at www.alicenter.org. Report your findings to the class.
2. Research one of Ali's famous fights. Make a poster to advertise the fight you chose.
3. Make a word web to show words that Muhammad Ali used to describe himself. Write a poem describing yourself.
4. Research the Sunni Muslim faith. Make a chart that describes Sunnis' beliefs.
5. Research the life and work of Malcolm X. Write a brief report on him and share it with the class.

Faith Ringgold

1. Find examples of Ringgold's story quilts online or in a book. Choose one that interests you. Write a paragraph explaining your impressions.
2. Obtain one of Faith Ringgold's children's books from your local library. Write a review of this book. Share it with the class.
3. Make a story quilt that portrays important events from your life. Use one block to portray each event. Tie the blocks together into a whole quilt.
4. Learn more about Faith Ringgold's foundation, the Anyone Can Fly Foundation, at www.artsnet.org/anyonecanfly. Choose one of the projects this foundation is undertaking. Describe the project to your class.

Alice Walker

1. Read one of Alice Walker's books, short stories, or poems. Give a summary to the class.
2. Watch the movie *The Color Purple*. Choose one of the characters in the movie. Write a description of the character you chose.
3. Research the voter registration drives that took place in Mississippi in the 1960s. Compare and contrast those efforts with voting and registration today.

Gladys Knight

1. Find out more about Gladys Knight. Create a newspaper article reporting your findings.
2. Learn more about diabetes. Access the American Diabetes Association Web site at www.diabetes.org. Create a brochure about diabetes.
3. Obtain a copy of Knight's book *At Home with Gladys Knight: Her Personal Recipe for Living Well, Eating Right, and Loving Life*. Make a recipe from the book.
4. Conduct research on another African-American singer. Write a recommendation or advertisement supporting the performer you chose.
5. Listen to one of Gladys Knight's songs. Give your impressions of the song to the class.

Bernice Johnson Reagon

1. Listen to music by Sweet Honey in the Rock. Analyze the music. Report your interpretation to the class.
2. Research an African-American gospel music composer and/or performer of your choice. Some examples are Charles Albert Tindley, Lucie E. Campbell, Thomas Andrew Dorsey, William Herbert Brewster, Roberta Martin, and Kenneth Morris. Report your findings to the class.
3. Choose a modern gospel musician. Play a song from this musician for the class. Explain why you selected the song.

Colin Powell

1. Conduct research on one of the international crises that Colin Powell worked to solve: Panama, Iraq's invasion of Kuwait, Kosovo, the Middle East, or the war on terrorism. Do you agree with the actions? Write a report to support your opinion.
2. Learn more about America's Promise at www.americaspromise.org. Choose a project to look into. Create an advertisement to promote the project you select.
3. Read Powell's autobiography, *My American Journey*.
4. Find out who the chairman of the Joint Chiefs of Staff and the U.S. Secretary of State are today. Use the Internet to learn about these people. Create a chart comparing and contrasting Colin Powell to each.
5. Use the Internet to learn more about ROTC. Explain why this type of program does or does not appeal to you.

Benjamin Carson

1. Research what is required to become a neurosurgeon. Summarize the requirements in an oral report.
2. Read one of Ben Carson's books: *THINK BIG*, *Gifted Hands*, or *The Big Picture*. Choose a chapter of the book. Write your opinion of the chapter.
3. Gather information about conjoined twins, including how they are formed, the classifications/types, and the history of conjoined twins. Summarize your findings in a report. Include a paragraph about one specific case you read about.
4. Develop your own rules for success. Make a poster to share your rules for success.
5. Ben Carson is a member of the Seventh-Day Adventist Church. Use the Internet to learn more about this group and its beliefs. Report your findings to the class. Investigate other religions and faiths. Choose one. Use a Venn diagram to compare and contrast the religion or faith you chose with the Seventh-Day Adventist Church.
6. Use the Internet to learn more about the Johns Hopkins School of Medicine. Explain your findings to the class.
7. Draw a diagram of the human brain.

Morgan Freeman

1. Watch one of Morgan Freeman's movies. Write a review of the movie. Or, give a spoken review to the class.
2. Create a map of Mississippi. Mark Clarksdale on the map. Illustrate the map with pictures of products/crops from the area.
3. Research famous blues singers from Mississippi. Find and listen to samples of their music. Create biographies of each one. Include illustrations.
4. Use the Internet to research Freeman's Rock River Foundation. Make a list of causes it supports.
5. Use the Internet to find a list of movies or plays Freeman has starred in. Make a list of those movies you have seen. Combine your results with those of the class and graph them.

Geoffrey Canada

1. Use the Internet to research the Harlem Children's Zone at www.hcz.org.
2. Compile your findings and write a report on what the Zone is doing today.
3. Investigate the progress at the Promise Academy at www.insideschools.org. Create a chart or graph to show the number of students and their average reading and math scores.
4. Geoffrey Canada has done much work with Marian Wright Edelman of the Children's Defense Fund. Use the Internet to research Edelman and her work. Give a brief report to the class.
5. Find out more about tai kwon do. Report on its basics to the class. Demonstrate or illustrate some techniques.

Ruth Simmons

1. Use the Internet to research Brown University. Give a summary of your findings to the class. Explain whether this university would be a good fit for you, and why.
2. Write a paragraph in which you describe the influence one of your teachers has had on your life.
3. Write a paragraph explaining why you think Ruth Simmons continues to search for disadvantaged minority students to attend Brown.

References

Langston Hughes

Bloom, Harold. *African-American Poets: Phillis Wheatley Through Melvin B. Tolson.* Philadelphia: Chelsea House Publishers, 2001.

Gable, Craig, ed. *Ebony Rising: Short Fiction of the Greater Harlem Renaissance Era.* Bloomington: Indiana University Press, 2004.

Raatma, Lucia. *Langston Hughes: African American Author and Poet.* Chanhassen, MN: The Child's World, 2002.

Rummel, Jack. *Langston Hughes, Poet.* Philadelphia: Chelsea House Publishers, 2005.

Jesse Owens

Gentry, Tony. *Jesse Owens: Champion Athlete.* Philadelphia: Chelsea House Publishers, 2005.

Herzog, Brad. *The 20 Greatest Athletes of the 20th Century.* New York: Rosen Publishing Group, 2002.

Owens, Jesse. *The Jesse Owens Story.* New York: Putnam, 1970.

Raatma, Lucia. *Jesse Owens: Track-and-Field Olympian.* Chanhassen, MN: The Child's World, 2003.

Schaap, Jeremy. *Triumph: The Untold Story of Jesse Owens and Hitler's Olympics.* Boston: Houghton Mifflin, 2007

Weatherford, Carole Boston. *Jesse Owens: Fastest Man Alive.* New York: Walker & Co., 2006

Benjamin O. Davis Jr.

Davis, Benjamin O., Jr. *Benjamin O. Davis, Jr.: American.* Washington, DC: Smithsonian Institution Press, 1991.

Gropman, Alan L. "Benjamin Davis, American." The Aviation History Online Museum, 2007. www.aviation-history.com/airmen/davis.htm.

Tuskegee Airmen, Inc. www.tuskegeeairmen.org.

Fannie Lou Hamer

Colman, Penny. *Fannie Lou Hamer and the Fight for the Vote.* Brookfield, CT: The Millbrook Press, 1993.

Mills, Kay. *This Little Light of Mine: The Story of Fannie Lou Hamer.* Lexington, KY: University Press of Kentucky, 2007.

Coretta Scott King

King, Coretta Scott. *My Life with Martin Luther King, Jr.* Rev. ed. New York: Henry Holt and Co., 1993.

Rhodes, Lisa Renee. *Coretta Scott King, Civil Rights Activist.* Legacy ed. Philadelphia: Chelsea House Publishers, 2005.

Vivian, Octavia. *Coretta: The Story of Coretta Scott King.* Minneapolis: Fortress Press, 2006.

Alex Haley

"Alex Haley." Contemporary Authors Online. Gale, 2003.

Haley, Alex. *Roots: The Saga of an American Family.* Garden City, New York: Doubleday & Co., 1976.

The Kunte Kinte-Alex Haley Foundation, Inc. www.kintehaley.org.

U.S.C.G.C. Alex Haley Web site. www.uscg.mil/pacarea/cgcAlexHaley.

Shirley, David. *Alex Haley, Author.* Philadelphia: Chelsea House Publishers, 2005.

Muhammad Ali

Ali, Muhammad. *The Greatest: My Own Story.* New York: Random House, 1975.

Ali, Muhammad, with Hana Yasmeen Ali. *The Soul of a Butterfly: Reflections on Life's Journey.* New York: Simon & Schuster, 2004.

Rummel, Jack. *Muhammad Ali: Heavyweight Champion.* Philadelphia: Chelsea House Publishers, 2004.

Faith Ringgold

"Faith Ringgold." www.randomhouse.com/kids/authors/#R.

Faith Ringgold's Web site. www.faithringgold.com.

Holton, Curlee Raven, and Faith Ringgold. *Faith Ringgold: A View From the Studio.* Piermont, NH: Bunker Hill Publishing, 2005.

Koolish, Lynda. *African American Writers: Portraits and Visions.* Jackson, MS: University Press of Mississippi, 2001.

Ringgold, Faith. *We Flew Over the Bridge: The Memoirs of Faith Ringgold.* Durham, NC: Duke University Press, 1995.

Alice Walker

Gentry, Tony. *Alice Walker, Author.* New York: Chelsea House Publishers, 1993.

Lazo, Caroline Evensen. *Alice Walker: Freedom Writer.* Minneapolis: Lerner Publications, 2000.

Raatma, Lucia. *Alice Walker: African-American Author and Activist.* Chanhassen, MN: The Child's World, 2003.

White, Evelyn C. *Alice Walker: A Life.* New York: Norton Publishing, 2004.

Gladys Knight

"Gladys Knight." *Contemporary Musicians,* Vol. 50. Farmington Hills, MI: Thomson Gale, 2005. Reproduced in *Biography Resource Center.* Farmington Hills, MI: Thomson Gale, 2008. www.gale.cengage.com/BiographyRC. (Specific articles are not available without subscription.)

"Gladys Knight and the Pips." www.rockhall.com.

"Gladys's Biography." www.aarp.org/fun/music/connections/gladys_knight_bio.html.

Knight, Gladys. *Between Each Line of Pain and Glory.* New York: Hyperion, 1998.

Nathan, David. *The Soulful Divas.* New York: Billboard Books, 1999.

Bernice Johnson Reagon

"Bernice Johnson Reagon." *Current Biography.* New York: H.W. Wilson, Co, 1999.

Bernice Johnson Reagon's Web Site. www.bernicejohnsonreagon.com.

Bessman, Jim. "Sweet Honey's Reagon Follows Path of the 'Singing Fighters'." *Billboard,* Vol. 114, No. 7, February 16, 2002, p. 38.

Kernan, Michael. "Conveying History Through Song." *Smithsonian,* Vol. 29, No. 11, February 1999, pp. 32–34.

Reagon, Bernice Johnson. *We'll Understand It Better By and By: Pioneering African American Gospel Composers.* Washington, DC: Smithsonian Institution Press, 1992.

Colin Powell

Brown, Warren. *Colin Powell: Soldier and Statesman.* Philadelphia: Chelsea House Publishers, 2005.

DeYoung, Karen. *Soldier: The Life of Colin Powell.* New York: Alfred A. Knopf, 2006.

Hinds, Patricia Mignon. *Essence: 50 of the Most Inspiring African-Americans.* New York: Essence Communications Partners and Time Inc. Home Entertainment, 2005.

Passaro, John. *Colin Powell: Journey to Freedom.* Chanhassen, MN: Child's World, 1999.

Powell, Colin. *My American Journey.* New York: Ballantine Books (Random House), 2005.

Benjamin Carson

Carson, Ben. *Gifted Hands: The Ben Carson Story.* Grand Rapids, MI: Zondervan, 1990.

Carson, Ben. *The Big Picture: Getting Perspective on What's Really Important in Life.* Grand Rapids, MI: Zondervan, 1999.

Carson, Ben. *THINK BIG: Unleashing Your Potential for Excellence.* Grand Rapids, MI: Zondervan, 1992.

Ben Carson's Web site: www.drbencarson.com.

Morgan Freeman

De Angelis, Gina. *Morgan Freeman.* Philadelphia: Chelsea House Publishers, 1999.

Griffin, Nancy. "Home Again." *AARP The Magazine.* November-December 2007, pp. 62–67.

"Morgan Freeman." *Contemporary Black Biography,* Vol. 20. Detroit: Gale Group, 1998. Reproduced in *Biography Resource Center.* Farmington Hills, MI: Thomson Gale, 2007. www.gale.cengage.com/BiographyRC. (Specific articles are not available without subscription.)

Tracy, Kathleen. *Morgan Freeman: A Biography.* Fort Lee, NJ: Barricade Books, 2006.

Geoffrey Canada

Canada, Geoffrey. *Fist Stick Knife Gun: A Personal History of Violence in America.* Boston: Beacon Press, 1995.

Canada, Geoffrey. *Reaching Up for Manhood: Transforming the Lives of Boys in America.* Boston: Beacon Press, 1998.

"Geoffrey Canada." *Contemporary Black Biography,* Vol. 22. Detroit: Gale Group, 1999. Reproduced in *Biography Resource Center.* Farmington Hills, MI: Thomson Gale, 2008. www.gale.cengage.com/BiographyRC. (Specific articles are not available without subscription.)

"Geoffrey Canada, Social Activist." *Current Biography,* February 2005. www.hwwilson.com/Currentbio/cover_bios/cover_bio_2_05.htm.

Pines, Deborah A. "America's Best Leaders: Thriving in the Zone." *U.S. News & World Report,* October 31, 2005, pp. 86–88.

Tough, Paul. "The Harlem Project." *The New York Times,* June 20, 2004. http://query.nytimes.com/gst/fullpage.html?res=9507E7D91030F933A15755C0A9629C8B63

Ruth Simmons

Clarke, Caroline V. *Take a Lesson: Today's Black Achievers on How They Made It and What They Learned Along the Way.* New York: John Wiley & Sons, 2001, pp. 193–200.

Crace, John. "Ruth Simmons: The Visible Woman." *The Guardian,* October 3, 2006. Available online at www.guardian.co.uk/education.

Kingsbury, Alex. "More Proof That Mentors Matter." *U.S. News & World Report.* Posted November 12, 2007 at http://www.usnews.com/articles/news/best-leaders/2007/11/12/ruth-j-simmons.html.

"Ruth J. Simmons." *Contemporary Black Biography,* Vol. 38. Farmington Hills, MI: Gale Group, 2003. Reproduced in *Biography Resource Center.* Farmington Hills, MI: Thomson Gale, 2007. www.gale.cengage.com/BiographyRC. (Specific articles are not available without subscription.)

"Ruth Simmons." *Notable Black American Women,* Vol. 3. Farmington Hills, MI: Gale Group, 2002. Reproduced in *Biography Resource Center.* Farmington Hills, MI: Thomson Gale, 2007. www.gale.cengage.com/BiographyRC. (Specific articles are not available without subscription.)

extending and enhancing learning

Let's stay in touch!

Thank you for purchasing these Walch Education materials. Now, we'd like to support you in your role as an educator. **Register now** and we'll provide you with updates on related publications, online resources, and more. You can register online at www.walch.com/newsletter, or fill out this form and fax or mail it to us.

Name _____ Date _____

School name _____

School address _____

City _____ State _____ Zip _____

Phone number (home) _____ (school) _____

E-mail _____

Grade level(s) taught _____ Subject area(s) _____

Where did you purchase this publication? _____

When do you primarily purchase supplemental materials? _____

What moneys were used to purchase this publication?

    [ ] School supplemental budget

    [ ] Federal/state funding

    [ ] Personal

[ ] Please sign me up for Walch Education's free quarterly e-newsletter, *Education Connection*.

[ ] Please notify me regarding free *Teachable Moments* downloads.

[ ] Yes, you may use my comments in upcoming communications.

COMMENTS _____

_____

_____

Please FAX this completed form to 888-991-5755, or mail it to:
Customer Service, Walch Education, 40 Walch Drive, Portland, ME 04103

www.walch.com

16 MORE Extraordinary African Americans